Cryptocurrency

Digital Revolution

By Edward T. Beckett

"I think the internet is going to be one of the major forces for reducing the role of government. The one thing that's missing but that will soon be developed, is a reliable e-cash."

- Professor Milton Friedman, a Nobel Prize winner in economics -
1999

Introduction

Bitcoin, Bitcoin, Bitcoin... you may have heard of it at this point. Is it the next era of money? Unlikely, but we can't know for certain. One thing is for sure. The technology behind these cryptocurrencies is permanent. And at the very least, based on the past, you could have already benefited from them a lot. Major changes are coming and you don't want to be left behind once it hits. This book will help you to understand digital currencies, benefits these currencies offer, and ideas where we are likely heading towards in the digital future.

First things first. Yes, Bitcoin and other cryptocurrencies have experienced incredible growth and media exposure in 2017 and then violent downwards movement in 2018. Anybody familiar with cryptos or Bitcoin most likely has some sort of opinion. Now if you have heard of Bitcoin by something like mainstream news, friends, family whatever, but never bothered to actually research it yourself, I can imagine you may be thinking something like: *"but it's already too late, Bitcoin is way too expensive for me. Anyway, it's going to crash."* Then after it goes down you are too afraid to buy again and in the worst case scenario later regret and buy in out of greed to not miss out. Bitcoin tends to act like traditional assets exaggerated by ten folds. By this statement I mean just like any asset class, Bitcoin goes through market cycles over the years but behaves far more aggressive. Compare the S&P 500 Index movement of **2016 $1860** to **2018 $2870** back to below **$2500**, against exactly the same three dates in Bitcoin price; **$397, $11 800,** and below **$4000**.

Here's some facts. The internet has by far made more millionaires in the last decade than any other medium. Even during the peak popularity of late 2017 , only roughly 1% of the total population of *internet users* own any cryptocurrency. Yes, 1%! Well, actually less than 1% as at the time of writing this book. Therefore, if only 1% of the total internet users own any Bitcoin, is it too late to join? What would the price of a single Bitcoin be if 5% of internet users started to use it? What if cryptocurrencies are eventually going to be perceived as a normal way of payment and money? Now here is where the speculation part easily carries over. In this book, you will learn all the advantages and disadvantages of digital money.

The very first digital currency Bitcoin promises quick peer to peer transactions, without the need for a middleman like bank. You may know Bitcoin, but have you ever heard of blockchain? Blockchain is the core technology that allows cryptocurrencies to function the way they do. I'm giving you this book as an unbiased starting point on your journey to the digital revolution. You may be surprised how rapidly our technology is evolving nowadays. As an early adopter there's also a lot of money to be made but let me be clear here. You need to know what you are doing. Read carefully through this book, and I can guarantee you will actually know way more about cryptocurrencies than the majority of people who own Bitcoin.

Okay. I keep repeating the word cryptocurrency. What is a cryptocurrency? Cryptocurrency is defined as a digital currency in which encryption is used to regulate the generation of units of the currency, verifying the transfer of funds, operating independently. What about the other cryptocurrencies, known as altcoins? If cryptocurrency gets really popular we can expect even altcoins worth pennies today be worth - who knows what- in near future. Many cryptocurrencies aren't even necessarily currencies, as their prime focus isn't to function as a currency. Who knows what great innovations there will be? Bitcoin as of now certainly isn't perfect, and its overall practical implementation into our daily lives like a regular currency is not there yet. What if an altcoin manages to solve all the major problems and actually replaces Bitcoin?

This is obviously just an unlikely speculation, but what would the price be if such happens? This is just an idea to make you think about the possibilities new technology brings with it. There's a lot of speculation when it comes to Bitcoin's future. Price predictions ranging from 0$ to 1,000,000$ per Bitcoin. You can find a bunch of theories & support for both.

Some topics in this book are somewhat simplified in order to give you a better understanding of cryptocurrency and its technology. Though we will touch some more advanced topics later on.

What can you expect?

First, I want to thank you for your interest in cryptocurrencies and for choosing my book. I hope you are open to the idea of this "imaginary internet money" as many perceive it at first. Yes, I will admit partly myself too. Well, after all, "dogecoin" is a legitimate currency with noticeable value, while having no actual development, so it's rather understandable I guess. Anyway, we have to keep in mind that everything changes. Not too long ago there wasn't even the concept of "money" as of a dollar. For example, when do you think was the first United States Dollar officially exchanged? Go and Google it and you will find out it was in 1792.

This book contains a clear, realistic introduction to the blockchain, giving you an idea of what it is and what it is being used for, what are the benefits before moving on to the future of the blockchain, cryptocurrencies, and why it has such potential. We will also take an honest review of all the major risks and

downsides of cryptocurrencies, helping you decide whether you want to be involved with them or not, hence we will go through arguments from both ends of the spectrum. It is difficult to find unbiased and factual (which is somewhat subjective anyway...) information on cryptocurrencies. Ask a person owning cryptocurrencies, which is the best cryptocurrency out there? They'll give the coin they own the most. But don't just take my word for it, learn things yourself, and remember... cryptocurrencies like everything else is merely a tool to manipulate consumer decisions in a way. Despite the benefits, it is still just another form of manipulation. Including this book. The difference however, is that Bitcoin, unlike the food, TV shows, social media etc. could actually greatly benefit you. Note the word *could*. And that is where this book comes into play.
Let's not already make things overcomplicated, we will go through the overcomplicated technical stuff more than enough. Still remember dogecoin? I actually checked for other rather "interesting" coins, and apparently, there are coins like, "pokecoin" ($0.000113 each) and "antiBitcoin" ($0.010013 each). Yes, you definitely should stay away from these types of coins, including many others.

When it comes to cryptocurrencies, there is a lot of misinformation out there. More specifically, we humans like to simplify things. It is okay to try and simplify the underlying ideas but try to remember there is also a lot of uncertainty with this technology, hence why we go through multiple different views, arguments and ideas. Our primary focus along with the currencies and Bitcoin will be on the blockchain, as it's the most important aspect to understand. Once you realize the concept of blockchain, you will better understand all the basics principles of Bitcoin and other cryptocurrencies. Finally, I will provide you with the basics and practical points on how to actually get into cryptocurrencies, as well as ideas and resources to learn more and optimize your income with them. Are cryptocurrencies a get-rich-quick scheme? One may ask. Actually, yes, they *kind* of are. Ready to do get rich? Hold on, you will have to read the book first. On a serious note though, let's begin.

Educating yourself on the topic of cryptocurrency and its technology as early as you can is absolutely crucial. Many have compared the current state of crypto money to the 1996~ state of the internet. Whatever the case, it's safe to assume at least few major cryptocurrencies are here to stay at this point. They simply provide too much benefits to be ignored completely. How relevant is Bitcoin going to be against a dollar in everyday life though? Nobody knows, but your best bet is to take time to understand the concept and then decide while we are still early, it is certain that blockchain will change the internet in some shape or form. So, if you are ready to learn, we are about to begin.

This book will refer to few different websites. I'd recommend to quickly glance at them as you are reading the book so you will start to grasp the bigger picture. For those interested on more resources. Once you are finished, look up the PDF enhancement file containing huge supply of resources and practical information.

Link to this file is located at the end of this book.

By Edward T. Beckett- All rights reserved.

This document is geared towards providing exact and reliable information in regards to the topic and issue covered. The publication is sold with the idea that the publisher is not required to render accounting, officially permitted, or otherwise, qualified services. If advice is necessary, legal or professional, a practiced individual in the profession should be ordered. The information presented herein represents mostly the view of the author as of the date of publication.

Due to the rate at which conditions change, the author reserves the right to alter and update his opinions based on new conditions & information. While every attempt has been made to verify the information in this book to be up to date, neither the author nor his affiliates assume any guaranteed responsibility for errors, inaccuracies or omissions due to extremely high rate at which this topic changes. In no way is it legal to reproduce, duplicate, or transmit any part of this document in either electronic means or in printed format. Recording of this publication is strictly prohibited and any storage of this document is not allowed unless with written permission from the publisher. All rights reserved.

I am not a qualified licensed investment advisor / financial guru, neither do I want to be one. All information found here, including any ideas, opinions, views, predictions, forecasts, commentaries, suggestions, value picks, are for informational or educational purposes only and should not be construed as personal investment advice nor instruction. Under no circumstances will any legal responsibility or blame be held against the publisher for any reparation, damages, or monetary loss due to the information herein, either directly or indirectly. Respective authors own all copyrights not held by the publisher.

The information herein is offered for informational purposes solely and is universal as so. The presentation of the information is without contract or any type of guarantee assurance. The trademarks that are used are without any consent, and the publication of the trademark is without permission or backing by the trademark owner. All trademarks and brands within this book are for clarifying purposes only and are the owned by the owners themselves, not affiliated with this document. Hopefully this encourages you to research on your own later.

Table of Contents

Introduction 2

Crypto Terms: Vocabulary 10

Chapter One: What Is Blockchain? 13

Chapter Two: The Future of Blockchain: Digital revolution 19

Chapter Three: Bitcoin vs. Ethereum 30

Chapter Four: It's a Scam 39

Chapter Five: Pros and Cons – The Story of Bitcoin 47

Chapter Six: Development of Money – Resisting Change 60

Chapter Seven: Digital Currency in 2020 - The Future of Money? ... 67

Chapter Eight: Practicality, the Digital Present 72

Chapter Nine: Long-Term Cryptocurrency assets 78

Chapter 10: How do I get Cryptocurrency? 94

Chapter 11: Digital Gold Mining 102

Chapter 12: Storing Your Cryptocurrency 108

Conclusion, What's Next? 118

Crypto Terms: Vocabulary

Throughout this book you may come across some unfamiliar terms. Actually, you will come across unfamiliar nonsense unless you are already exceptionally familiar with the topic. Here is some basic cryptocurrency, - blockchain, and - trading terms. You will miss a lot of the ideas if you skip this!

Cryptocurrency = Digital asset (aka. internet money if you will) designed to work as a tool of exchange using cryptography to secure the transactions and to control the unit supply of the currencies. There is a difference between actual cryptocurrencies (like Bitcoin, Litecoin & Monero), and projects (or companies) that utilize blockchain for specific purpose (like Ethereum).

Crypto assets = All the "cryptocurrencies" that utilize blockchain but do not aim to act as direct currencies like Bitcoin. They are more so like traditional stocks with additional blockchain benefits (examples; Ethereum, Cardano). However, for simplicity, I will still use the term cryptocurrency to describe all crypto assets.

Bitcoin = First worldwide decentralized cryptocurrency. Most dominant, valued and recognized coin.

Satoshi = Currently the smallest unit of a single Bitcoin recorded on blockchain. It's one hundred millionth of a bitcoin (0.00000001 BTC). Named after the creator of bitcoin. Just think of it as a cent of dollar pretty much. November 2017 1 US cent = 160 Satoshi. i.e. you can buy tiny fraction of a Bitcoin.

Altcoin = generally accepted name for any coin that isn't Bitcoin.

Address = Essentially same as home address. It's the location from which you receive, send, hold your currency. Basically bitcoin. These addresses are long and generally look like: "1MhN5qfH1vgx9CLL17i3DK9D2gzrHR7dZF"

Public & Private keys = Simplified, long numbers used as a key for receiving / sending data in the blockchain. Public key can be given to anyone, while private key is only for yourself to control the data. Basically: <u>Priv. Key -> Publ. Key -> Address</u>

Blockchain = Data system that allows the creation of digital ledger and transactions on a non-centralized network. Cryptography is the main operator allowing users to engage with the ledger without any central operator, creating complete transparency. Basically, the main reason around all the hype around cryptocurrencies.

Block = Essential pages in a ledger or records. Blocks are the files where unalterable data related to the network is stored. Forever.

Block Reward = reward allotted for solving the mathematical equation related to a block.

Mining = Discovering and solving a block in the blockchain. Reward is given for solving the block and lengthening the chain. **Bitcoin blockchain** reward is bitcoins divided between all the different miners. Keeps the network running.

Difficulty = Determines how difficult it is to hash a new **block**. Basically, the lower the number, the harder it's to produce enough hash to solve the **block**.

Fork = Very simply put, they are upgrades to the current version of the **Blockchain**. For example, one fork into the bitcoin blockchain was supposed to happen in November 2017.

Hashrate = The speed at which a block is discovered -> rate the math problem is solved to gain the reward and lengthening the blockchain.

Smart Contract = Contract between two individuals stored on the blockchain. Simply put almost like a real-world contract. Except once signed into the blockchain, can't be altered. Practically: send bitcoin, bye bitcoin. No revokes, no central authority.

Basic terms good to know

Asset = Resource expected to provide future benefit
Crypto Exchanges = Institution, organization allowing you to interact with cryptocurrencies for a fee.
Portfolio = Collection of all your investments
Diversification = Reducing the risk of investment by purchasing assets in different sectors.
Limit Order = Buy or sell at a specified price for purchase to happen.
Long/Short =Simplified, they are often referred to long, buying/short, selling.
Dip =Opinion that X coin's price decrease is just temporary i.e. coin X is down 15% for the day.
Bullish/Bearish = Price will increase over time, bullish. Price will decline, bearish.
FOMO = Fear of missing out, quite common in cryptocurrencies since market is often driven by emotion, speculation and highly volatile short-term returns. i.e. specific crypto gains 10,20,30% in value, you start to fear you're missing out on something big. **Never** ideal state to buy any asset.
Market cycles = market cycles are the long-term price patterns of stock markets often associated with general business cycles. Understand, markets always move in cycles. What comes up must come down so they say. Can be identified as long-term bullish growth and long-term bearish descent repeating itself over and over again.

Chapter One: What Is Blockchain?

It is 560 BC. Imagine that you are a general of an army planning to attack an enemy city, the city is ancient but it has strong defense. You have the enemy city surrounded by several different battalions. Each of them led by a different general. A coordinated attack by all the forces would lead to a flawless victory. However, an uncoordinated attack would likely lead to either a defeat or heavy losses. You plan to attack by the dawn. You neither have a phone nor internet connection. (could you imagine that...) Creating signals may be seen by the enemy. How can you be sure that all the other battalions will come to the consensus to attack together by dawn? You could send messengers, but each party would need multiple messengers to verify the message completely, since one of the messengers could be captured and replaced by the enemy to deliver a fake message. Or one of the battalions could be lying, and once the rest of the army is attacking, one battalion retreats resulting in a defeat. How can you ever be absolutely sure that all the battalions trust each other and attack by dawn?

Now imagine that the battalions are actually computers on a network and the generals are computer programs running on a ledger. Ledger that records everything into a blockchain in the exact way the events occur. If anything is proven to be true by the blockchain's algorithm, it's immediately being informed to every other ledger equally. In conclusion, a decentralized technology always making sure everything is in consensus based on math, never seen before in human history. We don't know how far this technology will evolve. For now, it's been mainly focused around digital currencies like Bitcoin and other cryptocurrencies.

The blockchain is the most revolutionary technology to ever see the light of day, and it first came about through Bitcoin, the cryptocurrency designed and released by Satoshi Nakamoto in 2009. Bitcoin was the very first cryptocurrency that worked, the first that eliminated the issue of double spending and the first truly decentralized monetary system ever to see the light of day. It was also the first to introduce a blockchain that really worked, and this is what we are going to be looking at – the blockchain, how Bitcoin and Ethereum, the two most popular cryptocurrencies, compare to one another, and some tips on investing in cryptocurrencies, not to mention where the blockchain is headed. Bitcoin is believed to be merely the "generation one" of the entire blockchain era. All the cryptocurrencies operate under blockchain. Blockchain has received a lot of attention lately and is being developed rapidly.

The blockchain is the one subject that you will hear being talked about, everywhere you look or go. It may be the most talked about subject of all time, but it is also one of the most misunderstood. The blockchain is completely revolutionizing the way we carry out digital transactions, and it could very well change the way that some industries operate.

Blockchain and Bitcoin are two words that have fast become accepted every-day vocabulary. The two words do tend to be used interchangeably, but they shouldn't be because they are two different things. Related they may be, but Bitcoin refers to a virtual currency, one we hear termed as cryptocurrency while the blockchain is the technology that Bitcoin operates on.

Bitcoin is a decentralized currency, one that lets people exchange money or other value without the need for an intermediary to get involved. Every transaction made is logged, verified by the peers on the network, and placed onto the public ledger, the blockchain. This is what ensures that every transaction is authentic and stops fraud. It is the blockchain that facilitates each transaction, cutting out the need to have a third party.

One of the biggest benefits of the blockchain is its transparency. The ledger is a fully functional chronicle detailing every transaction on the ledger, right back to the first block, called the genesis block. Every time a transaction happens, like one person sending Bitcoin to another, all the details of the transaction, including the transaction source, the destination, the date, and time-stamp are all added into what is called a block.

This block has every transaction that has been verified within a set time-frame, currently 10 minutes for Bitcoin. These time intervals will vary between cryptocurrencies with some boasting block times of merely seconds. The transactions within the block are checked by the miners on the network using their combined computing power.

Individually, the miners are computers that are specifically set up to use their CPU and GPU cycles to solve mathematical algorithms. Once the algorithm has been solved, that block and all the transactions contained in it are confirmed as legitimate, and it is added to the blockchain. Simplified, the miner who solves the problem is rewarded with a certain amount of Bitcoin (12.5 at the moment). Each block contains something called a hash which contains a link to the previous block, thus linking each block irrevocably. As well as being updated constantly, the blockchain and all the blocks on it are distributed across all the computers on the network, and this is what ensures that the most up to date version is in existence everywhere thereby making it just about impossible to forge.

Why Do We Need a Blockchain?

It allows so many new possibilities. Most of us will have heard of Peer2Peer. It's been around for a long time in many different formats and it is what allows us to distribute digital assets between parties. Torrent sites use P2P for the distribution of files, movies, books, etc., for example. But one question that pops up here, why do we need the blockchain if we can already do all of this?

The answer to that lies in the way the Bitcoin blockchain works. Just imagine, just for a minute, that there was no blockchain. You own a single Bitcoin that has an identifier that links it to you. Now, let's imagine that you wanted to purchase a television, and the provider you choose accepts cryptocurrency as a payment method. Your chosen television just happens to cost, yep, 1 Bitcoin.

However, you also have to pay your friend back the Bitcoin that he lent you last month. With no blockchain in place, you could quite easily pay your friend and buy the television, and this is what we call double-spending – the same coin gets spent twice, and someone is going to be out of pocket! It is for this reason that P2P transactions never really caught on until recently. With the blockchain in place, the public record of every transaction gets distributed to each peer, and each transaction block is confirmed before the transactions contained in it can be made final, and that eliminates all the risks of double spending.

Up until now, we have had to put our faith and trust in third parties, messengers like the banks and credit card companies, to make sure our transactions were validated and that everything was above board. For that "privilege," you get charged a fee by the third party. With the blockchain, you can transfer your digital assets from place to another without having to go through that middleman, knowing full well that your money is safe and that there are security checks in place. Basically, you are in control. Not the middleman. Not to mention where the blockchain is headed, Bitcoin is believed to be just the "generation one" of the underlying blockchain era.

You won the battle. The army came to consensus and the battalions attacked together. This is because they understood the utility of consensus. If this was your first time reading about the technology, please take your time and read this chapter for a second time if needed, because this is the essential part of the technology where it is all based on.

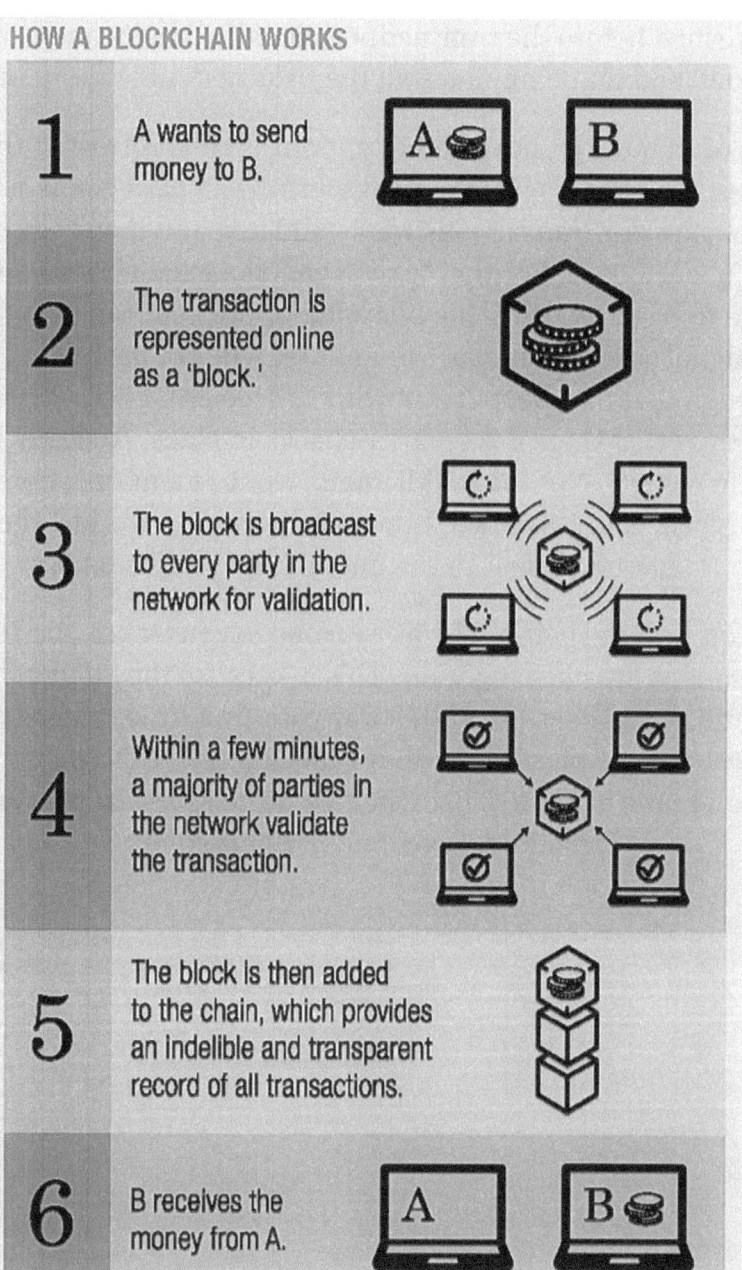

Chapter Two: The Future of Blockchain: Digital revolution

It is very likely that our financial futures are going to be dominated by the blockchain, simply because having a global currency that can be traced from the day it was mined right through every owner, together with one of the most efficient and effective infrastructures ever seen, will bring incredible results in reducing costs for everybody. Expect cryptocurrencies like Bitcoin to do for the finance industry what email and instant messaging have done for the world of communication. We basically call projects operating on the blockchain crypto**currencies**, because the original idea of Bitcoin was to be virtual open-source currency. However, over the past years we have realized that the blockchain technology has so much more potential than just being a currency. If I were to tell you in 2005, that an app cutting out taxis (the middleman), is going to be worth billions of dollars in the near future, would you believe it? As we know, Uber did it. So did Netflix. Perhaps the definition of a middleman is not carved in store but it is quite similar to what blockchain aims to solve.

What Can We Expect to See?

Quite a lot! The banks could slowly start adopting the major cryptocurrencies like Bitcoin or developing their own local cryptocurrency. We can expect to see much wider use of currencies secured by cryptography. As well, we can also expect to see the technology expand into the stock markets and equity management etc.

Many believe that the decentralizing force (cutting the middleman) could be one of the next big trends. After all, the recent Facebook data "scandal" combined with few other similar cases have turned more and more people against the current big providers like Facebook and Google. Although the blockchain at its current state does not solve everything, it is certainly a step in the right direction.

Which industries do you think could be "Ubered" next? – that is, transformed into a peer-to-peer industry conducted on an app. The conclusion at Parallel Polis – and in Silicon Valley – is that any industry that takes a cut of a deal between two people or holds fixed assets that can be provided informally will be "Ubered" at some point in the future, because smartphones link buyers and sellers directly. Other changes that are entirely possible include:

- A reduction in cyber-risks because of a better way of authenticating identity on a public ledger

- Smart contracts for car rental agencies – built on the blockchain, these contracts would allow a rental automatically on receipt of payment in cryptocurrency and confirmation of insurance through the trustless nature of blockchain records.

- Blockchain-connected refrigerators and freezers that communicate via the internet to the external world for the purposes of warranty tracking, upgrades to the software and even ordering groceries and paying for them.

- It is possible that smaller businesses could create trusted platforms for trading among themselves
- The blockchain has the potential to bring transparency and robustness to the post-trade environment
- Banks could make payments to suppliers instantly across the internet
- One new startup on the blockchain is claiming that their software will help to track criminals down much faster and at a lower cost than before
- The blockchain has the potential to replace the central banks entirely
- The blockchain technology could cut the costs of cross-border payments, regulatory compliance, and securities trading by up to $20 billion by the year 2022.
- Applications in and external to the banks may be reduced because the blockchain transactions have got all the information needed for transfers of assets and/or the contracts related to them
- Bitcoin and some of the other cryptocurrencies may end up dominating finance in many nations across the world.
- The blockchain has the potential to reduce lenders' settlements by up to $20 billion a year
- Many industries are starting to realize that one of the biggest innovations of the blockchain is in its capability to reduce or even cut out completely trusted middlemen

in any transaction
(charities, elections, energy, insurance, accounting, real-estate, music, networks, healthcare and so many more)

- The blockchain has the potential to disrupt existing processes and technologies while creating new ones at the same time
- Artificial intelligence, by moving the artificial machine learning systems into blockchain, in fact both technologies benefit. The use of blockchain technology could increase artificial trust, effectiveness, and reduce risks.
- The blockchain will shrink the world because it can increase the speed and the efficiency of transactions
- Blockchain technology has the potential to transform the distribution of social welfare in some of the developing nations
- Elections could in the future be run on the blockchain, eliminating fraud and cutting costs
- Blockchain could even help to fight climate change by bringing transparency to the energy industry as well as possibly countless of other corrupted fields

Other Use Cases:

Distributed Cloud Storage

In the next few years, data storage on the blockchain will become a huge disruptor. Right now, the cloud storage that we use is centralized and you are placing your trust for security of your data in the hands of one provide, giving them control of your assets. With the blockchain, this is decentralized. Some storage plans are already in beta testing and more are expected to follow.

Digital Identity

Digital security is a huge concern the world over and estimates of the cost to the industry stand at around $18.5 billion every year which means that, for every $3 spent, $1 goes to fraud. The blockchain makes the business of tracking digital identities and managing them more efficient and secure, resulting in much fewer instances of fraud.

The blockchain technology is offering a solution to a good many of the issues that surround digital identity, solutions where the identity can be authenticated in an immutable, irrefutable and secure way. At the moment, we use passwords and we store them on systems that are not especially secure. An identity system based on the blockchain uses digital signatures which are, in turn, based on secure public key cryptography. The only check that needs to be carried out is whether the transaction is signed by the right key and the inference is that whoever has the private key is the owner – exact identity is not relevant.

Use cases include:

This kind of technology can be used for the application of identity management and authentication in these areas:

- Passports
- Digital identities
- E-Residency
- Wedding certificates
- Birth certificates
- Death certificates
- IDs

And limitless innovation possibilities without asking anyone's permission!

One example is called Sho-card – a digital identity that provides protection for consumer privacy It is incredibly easy to understand and is as easy to use as showing an ID card or driving license. It has been fully optimized for use on a mobile and its security level is so high that even the banks can rely on it. There is also development outside of blockchain. Very similar technologies with modified systems. Once these systems are launched to the public, they are still likely to be listed as cryptocurrencies.

Evolution of Internet

How did the internet we know today evolve? The first-generation World Wide Web or "web 1.0" started being available to the public during the early nineties. It was based on the simple HTML format, allowing computers to share and browse different documents. The first-generation web was all about efficient information, with practically little to no interaction between users as we know today, some may remember the era of MSN messenger. Would you have agreed back in 2000 that people sharing pranks online would be 10 times richer than a doctor or professor with decades of education & experience? On a side note even though I somewhat despise the predictions like: *"this cryptocurrency will be worth "X" in January 26th of 2021"* or the legendary *"Bitcoin is going to a million dollars by 2020"*, some of them **may** end up being somewhere near the truth after all. Making predictions on a speculative asset is quite fun of course. Bitcoin could indeed be worth 10 million dollars the next year. (almost serious prediction) Anyhow throughout the early 2000s, the technology evolved enabling developers to build different applications, like Amazon, Facebook, Instagram, YouTube, Google and even live streaming where people could directly write, sell, and share data on. Without specific technical understanding. This completely revolutionized the user interface, allowing huge mass adoption. While keeping the efficient share of information, "web 2.0" allowed diverse interaction through different social media platforms. Creating the web 2.0 or simply put, the internet we all know and use right now.

Decentralized Web 3.0

While the web 2.0 democratized many power structures creating opportunities for many, it slowly grew highly centralized around the biggest private networks. Highly centralized environment created many issues such as security, privacy, and control all in the hands of huge enterprises with their personal motives. Let's take a look at an example. Have you ever wondered how the ads you often see are quite precise? This is because these biggest enterprises have the ability to access all of your personal data, allowing them to design specific ads for specific target audience. Or how you often have to follow specific instructions before being able to use a service.

Through the recent rise and discovery of blockchain technology, the idea of decentralized web 3.0 has actually started to become a real possibility. The vision for this decentralized web is to return the power back to the people, as the initial purpose of internet. Unlike Bitcoin or many other cryptocurrencies, these projects are looking to be on a different niche. Leaving the coins of these projects to act as more of a company shares rather than direct currency. What is the big deal of this decentralized web? The next generation web will most likely be a combination of all the latest technology such as blockchain, distributed web, IPFS (peer-to-peer protocol specifically designed for decentralized web) and IoT (internet of things). Now we are going to look at some of the biggest advantages web 3.0 technology brings:

- **No central control:** Middlemen are removed from the equation, just like with Bitcoin allows peer-to-peer trades, the decentralized platforms like Ethereum and EOS are providing a trust-less platform where the rules are unbreakable and data is encrypted. Enterprises like, Google and Apple will no longer have control of all the users.

- **No government or single entity** can kill the services and sites on will.

- **Data is decentralized:** End users will remain in complete control of their data and security.

- **Uninterrupted service:** Account suspension and distributed denial of service are reduced substantially.

- **Open source** access and interaction with the network, like Bitcoin

- **Hack and data gap reduction** by improved security

- **Adaptive:** Machine learning and artificial intelligence services allow more personalized applications

Although the underlying core infrastructure is there, the move towards web 3.0 will likely take many years. Emerging technology is likely to refine, as we have witnessed in the previous development of web 1 & 2. After the infrastructure has been established, the friendly user interface and adoption will follow.

Just a few examples. Nothing is certain, but the decentralized web is developing. Since these "dapps" are built upon the operating system, it is likely to emerge competition between the service providers, like Ethereum, EOS, Cardano and many others. The competition between these operating systems has been growing rapidly.

The blockchain may appear to be a fad to many people but much of that is down to a lack of understanding. As more and more uses for the technology are brought to the forefront, we can expect to see some radical changes in the near future. During the early days of internet, many authorities claimed, "nobody is ever going to use this." Next, you will learn more about the basics of Bitcoin and Ethereum as well as their differences. You will also find out what separates a crypto**currency** from a blockchain based infrastructure.

"Over the next decade, there will be disruption as significant as the internet was for publishing, where blockchain is going to disrupt dozens of industries, one being capital markets and Wall Street".

- Patrick M. Byrne

Chapter Three: Bitcoin vs. Ethereum

Although we date Bitcoin back to 2009, it was 10 years earlier, in 1999, that Milton Friedman, the Nobel Prize winner for economics, said, "I think the internet is going to be one of the major forces for reducing the role of government. The one thing that's missing, but that will soon be developed, is a reliable e-cash."

Ten years later, we got Bitcoin, Ethereum and even the possibility for countless of other industries to evolve in the future, including the internet itself. Although there are thousands of cryptocurrencies now, Bitcoin has remained the dominant force, becoming the single largest blockchain network in the entire world. Until Ethereum was born. Developed by Vitalik Buterin, Ethereum takes a different path to Bitcoin, a path that includes the cryptocurrency but is not limited to it. Bitcoin and Ethereum are similar when you first look at them, but go a little deeper, and you will start to see some big differences. Now that you understand how the blockchain works, it is time to dig deeper on the biggest existing projects currently utilizing the technology.

Bitcoin

Satoshi Nakamoto, the creator of Bitcoin, is an anonymous person or group of people who first released open-source white paper digital currency named Bitcoin in 2008. That paper described Bitcoin and what it was for, followed by the launch of the cryptocurrency the following year.

At that time, the Bitcoin exchange rate was $1 per 1,209.02 Bitcoin, and that rate came about after the cost of the electricity to run the computers that generated the currency was worked out. The very first Bitcoin transaction that we know about was when Laszlo Hanyecz from Florida purchased two Papa John pizzas for 10,000 Bitcoin – at the time that equated to around $30. Today, that 10,000 Bitcoin would be worth in the region of $97,000,000 (ninety-seven million). Ouch, let's hope it was his cheat day or something and those 100 million pizzas were really good.

Bitcoin was the currency associated with the very first blockchain, and there are several reasons why Bitcoin quickly rose in popularity:

- **Privacy** – The history of any Bitcoin transaction, from the day it was created to the current date, is visible for anyone to see it. We can all see the entire history of a specific Bitcoin if we wish to. However, what you can't see, and this is down to the Bitcoin protocol, is any identifying information about the owner of a Bitcoin. So you can't associate any Bitcoin with any specific person. That protects the privacy of the owner, and all transactions happen autonomously. This also made early Bitcoin popular among criminals.

- **No Inflation** – The total number of Bitcoin that will ever be created has been capped at 21 million, completely different from the fiat currency we use now. Inflation happens when dollar decreases in value because of an increase in supply, usually when the government prints more money. This can't happen with Bitcoin, and because of the cap, it will remain in scarce circulation.

- **No Central Authority.** Bitcoin is the first truly open protocol that lets people freely transact with no central authority to govern it, and this provides autonomy. Bitcoin is also arguably the most decentralized cryptocurrency in the world.

- **It's faster** – The transactions happen within minutes whenever you transfer your Bitcoin to someone - even though there's plenty of room to improve the transactions. Some altcoins like Litecoin, have improved the transaction speed. However, one of Bitcoin's biggest issues is the fact that its current network can't seem to handle a large number of users very well, which has led to discussions on whether or not Bitcoin can be the everyday currency for everyone. This required new solution for the Bitcoin scaling issue, currently known as lightning network.

- **Secure** – Bitcoin is one of the most secure cryptocurrencies due to its huge network. It is backed by open source code.

The Bitcoin Goal

Bitcoin has the goal of acting as a secure P2P payment system that is decentralized. Because each transaction is on a ledger, any user can relax with the confidence that all transactions are legitimate, and they don't have to worry about fraudulent activity. The top priority is security, closely followed by speed. Any transaction will appear on the system within a matter of minutes and because it uses C++for coding, which has less than 70 commands, it is secure. When it comes to trust, anybody can see the source code of Bitcoin on Github.com. For those of us who are not developers however, it looks like a bunch of nonsense.

Bitcoin currency is placed into circulation through mining. This is the process of distributing the transaction information through the network, validating each one and putting it onto the blockchain. Each miner will receive a fee for each transaction that they validate and place into a block successfully. In short, they use their computer processing power to complete all the transactions and are given Bitcoin as a reward. However, nowadays these computers require a lot more processing power due to increased mining difficulty on Bitcoin. It's only considerable on a specific miner. We will get back to this in chapter 10.

"Bitcoin will do to banks what email did to the postal industry."

- Rick Falkvinge, Founder of the Swedish pirate party

Ethereum

You just got through Bitcoin, and you are confused? Don't worry, now you will get even more confused. Where Bitcoin is a system of decentralized digital payment, Ethereum is more of an infrastructure. For a basic understanding, think of infrastructure as the operating system of a smartphone or computer but in the blockchain. It is relatively new, only coming into existence in 2015. Don't get confused whenever someone is calling Ethereum or other infrastructure-based projects cryptocurrencies like Cardano. The cryptocurrency coin offered is called Ether, and it had an initial offering of 60 million Ethers, the sale of which raised around $18.5 million. While in

Ethereum's case the coin does act somewhat as a currency, it is still rather closer to a speculative company share. This applies to the majority of cryptocurrencies with the current low adoption. Holding the coin itself obviously means you are betting for the project to succeed. Right from the start, Ethereum was strongly supported, but what does make it so different to Bitcoin?

Ethereum was also the first project to offer something else – smart contracts. The goal behind a smart contract is usually to decentralize a centralized or federated service in order to improve transparency and reduce the need for trust through the use of blockchain technology. On top of that, in many cases you actually gain a lot of economic efficiency, because you no longer need to pay central actor to do something. Great real-life example for the use of a basic smart contract would be lottery. The Ethereum protocol was built to provide more flexibility and to provide more functionality to developers, and this pushes the boundaries of the traditional P2P currencies like Bitcoin. It also provides a new format for the traditional one that we associate with Kickstarter and other crowdsourcing platforms.

Many startup businesses use platforms like Kickstarter to try to generate money for their business, but these platforms are not free of cons, including a site fee of % and a payment processing fee of between 3 and 5%. Together, this can add up to around 10% of any funds generated for the startup.

By contrast, Ethereum lets people use the existing infrastructure and technology to raise their funds. For example, when a new project is started, a contract can be created and pledges sought from the community. A project goal is created, and the amount of funds needed to get the project off the ground is set. Any money raised will be held until the goal is met or a previously agreed date is reached. If for example, the project did not meet the monetary goal by the date, the system would be programmed to release any funds directly back to the correct contributors on another specified date within the contract.

This approach is incredibly streamlined and lets users leverage the blockchain to organize their funding efficiently while eliminating the fees generally associated with other crowdfunding platforms. If you didn't understand anything, don't worry, just read it again or simply think of Ethereum as a company that you can buy shares of (Ether 450$) for now.

Bitcoin does not have this functionality, and one other interesting thing about the Ethereum blockchain technology is that it generates a brand-new kind of organizational structure that helps people to get their ideas off the ground much quicker.

For example, let's assume that you have generated enough funding for a brand-new business idea. As soon as the funds are made available, you can go ahead and get the proposals from those who backed your project. When these have all been collected, every person who contributed would be given one vote that will help to generate the best way forward. No one person is given the job of making any decisions about the company's future; it is a collaboration which breaks away from the traditional structure of top-down management.

The usual task of hiring managers to complete paperwork and make decisions is pushed aside and an automated system takes its place, with a set of rules pre-programmed to keep things moving. This approach keeps the project protected from external influence, keeps the network decentralized, shuts down on downtime, and gets the project moving fast.

The Major Differences

Now you know how each platform works, let's look at some of the main differences between the two types of blockchain technology:

- **Different block times.** Bitcoin averages around 10 minutes whereas Ethereum is working on a block time of 12 seconds. However, although Ethereum is much faster, they also have more orphaned blocks – these are blocks that are created when two peers find a block simultaneously and one is discarded.

- **Supply of money.** Already, around two-thirds of the available Bitcoin supply has been mined, and the vast majority of those were awarded to the early miners. Ethereum, on the other hand, raised the capital they needed at a presale, and by the time it has been in existence for 5 years, it is expected that only half of its total supply will be mined. For Bitcoin, the reward for mining halves every four years of 210,000 blocks but Ethereum miners are rewarded on the Ethash proof-of-work algorithm, whereby 5 Eth are given for each block. And Ethereum has no cap on total supply.

- **Transaction costs.** Bitcoin transactions are limited to the size of the blocks, whereas Ethereum uses 'gas' to fuel each transaction and the cost will vary depending on the complexity and storage requirements of the transaction and use of the bandwidth.

- **Differences in coding.** Ethereum is supposedly blockchain infrastructure, while Bitcoin is store of value or a currency. Ethereum uses code which is Turing-complete, and this lets anything is calculated provided there are sufficient time and computing power. While this has advantages, it also brings with it certain complications and may well be partly responsible for the June 2017 DAO hack where a major attack was executed on a company that uses the system. That thief took off with $50 million, and this pushed the price of one unit down to $15 from $21.50 in just a few hours. Since then developers have come up with a fix that they claim will stop the attacker and prevent any of the stolen funds from being used or spent. This event shows us what is possible when a system has vulnerabilities in it. The reason could be attributed to the attempted centralization of a decentralized system, something that Bitcoin does not do.

Moving Forward, Litecoin and altcoins

Many people compare Bitcoin and Ethereum, and although they have similar technology, each has very different goals. Bitcoin has a proven track record as a cryptocurrency while Ethereum is closing the gap with a different kind of technology. Not only can you use the blockchain technology to carry out transactions, you can also create contracts and execute them as well as generate startup funding. But, while they differ in many ways, they do have one identical shared goal – to meet the needs of the user. To do that, they will need to evolve as the needs of the user will evolve and the technology has got to keep up. Therefore, Bitcoin and Ethereum are detached from each other.

However, many of the altcoins are currencies and therefore very similar to Bitcoin, making them direct competition. Like Coke vs. Pepsi.

For example, Litecoin. Litecoin is very similar to Bitcoin in terms of use cases. Many like to perceive Bitcoin as gold and Litecoin as silver. So, what does Litecoin exactly offer making it worthy of note?

- Faster transactions, utilizes more technology.
- Easier to mine and with about4 times the supply of Bitcoin. Bigger supply could mean it's easier to adopt as an actual currency, rather than an asset like gold for instance.
- Doesn't use the same proof-of-work / mining algorithm Bitcoin has, so it isn't directly competing for miners
- Arguably undervalued due to Bitcoin's highlight.
- Charlie Lee is Litecoin's creator, publicly known and clear director of Litecoin. Promoting Litecoin's message clearly for the masses. However drastically reducing the decentralized aspect of the coin.
- Downside is the rather close dependence on Bitcoin's success. Essentially, there can only be one Bitcoin. Yet even Bitcoin is not widely used for practical purposes.

Chapter Four: It's a Scam

Now I'd like you to take a moment and look at:

Cryptocurrencies: 1334 / Markets: 7220   Market Cap: $430,195,269,914 / 24h Vol: $35,203,316,409 / BTC Dominance: 62.1%

Cryptocurrency Market Capitalizations

Market Cap ▼ Trade Volume ▼ Trending ▼ Tools ▼   Search Currencies

All Cryptocurrencies

Market Cap: All   Price: All   Volume (24h): All

All ▼ Coins ▼ Tokens ▼   USD ▼   ← Back

#	Name	Symbol	Market Cap	Price	Circulating Supply	Volume (24h)	% 1h	% 24h
1	Bitcoin	BTC	$266,938,062,759	$15,957.00	16,728,587	$21,182,100,000	0.94%	-4.71%
2	Ethereum	ETH	$44,259,254,909	$459.99	96,217,654	$2,362,090,000	0.88%	5.48%
3	Bitcoin Cash	BCH	$25,044,380,465	$1,486.77	16,844,825	$2,579,340,000	0.76%	10.24%
4	IOTA	MIOTA	$12,446,958,970	$4.48	2,779,530,283 *	$856,395,000	0.94%	7.89%
5	Ripple	XRP	$9,969,712,622	$0.257355	38,739,144,847 *	$871,062,000	1.41%	12.97%
6	Litecoin	LTC	$7,034,411,410	$129.77	54,205,508	$1,476,390,000	0.30%	32.03%
7	Dash	DASH	$5,783,280,818	$747.06	7,741,398	$290,538,000	0.76%	8.12%
8	NEM	XEM	$4,538,493,000	$0.504277	8,999,999,999 *	$169,402,000	-5.16%	104.95%
9	Monero	XMR	$4,320,439,497	$279.65	15,449,232	$205,900,000	1.10%	0.09%
10	Bitcoin Gold	BTG	$4,310,998,562	$258.21	16,695,449	$185,122,000	-1.63%	-1.25%
11	Cardano	ADA	$2,986,072,568	$0.115172	25,927,070,538 *	$69,109,000	1.70%	1.38%
12	Ethereum Classic	ETC	$2,815,853,584	$28.67	98,205,754	$555,172,000	0.87%	3.17%
13	NEO	NEO	$2,413,268,000	$37.13	65,000,000 *	$123,376,000	1.09%	4.92%

December 2017

#	Name	Symbol	Market Cap	Price
1	Bitcoin	BTC	$6,487,950,808	$431.4
2	XRP	XRP	$202,989,110	$0.00605
3	Litecoin	LTC	$153,184,845	$3.4
4	Ethereum	ETH	$72,409,494	$0.95327
5	Dash	DASH	$19,820,453	$3.2
6	Dogecoin	DOGE	$15,091,783	$0.00014
7	Peercoin	PPC	$9,788,940	$0.42773
8	BitShares	BTS	$8,687,533	$0.00342
9	Stellar	XLM	$8,386,835	$0.00173
10	Nxt	NXT	$7,329,199	$0.00732

January 2016

#	Name	Market Cap	Price	Volume (24h)
1	Bitcoin	$63,751,978,647	$3,646.07	$5,458,313,801
2	XRP	$13,450,958,429	$0.327749	$443,301,303
3	Ethereum	$12,875,966,150	$123.32	$2,875,444,592
4	Bitcoin Cash	$2,275,173,374	$129.49	$164,870,129
5	EOS	$2,205,767,205	$2.43	$704,997,420
6	Stellar	$2,049,482,674	$0.107151	$93,070,058
7	Tether	$2,031,591,504	$1.02	$4,004,949,452
8	Litecoin	$1,911,019,387	$31.83	$545,111,807
9	TRON	$1,659,312,534	$0.024896	$190,009,612
10	Bitcoin SV	$1,358,392,920	$77.32	$68,123,799
11	Cardano	$1,158,419,669	$0.044680	$36,332,398

And January 2019

(source: coinmarketcap.com, one of many websites providing historical price data)

Cryptocurrency Wild West

Welcome back. So, what do you think? It's pretty messy at first, isn't it? Some call it the digital wild west. Quite precise at the moment, but how long did the non-rule era of Wild West last? Perhaps we don't settle our arguments with a duel to death... yet. As you can see, there are over a thousand different cryptocurrencies. Of which, almost all are practically worthless. Depending whom you are talking to, the opinions vary. Some may say only Bitcoin is real, and everything else is a scam. While someone else is only invested in the "penny coins." Others may say all cryptocurrencies are useless. I can't give you an exact answer. You will have to search around to see which coins if any, you want to be associated with. It should definitely be noted that the vast majority of cryptocurrency projects are either useless or flat scams long-term. After all, Bitcoin is the only steady cryptocurrency thus far (always been the biggest). Researching each project carefully before making assumptions is by far the most important part.

If you are a beginner or never even heard of Bitcoin before this book, and you are considering to get some cryptocurrency, stick to Bitcoin until you get more familiar with the technology and market in general. Bitcoin's USD price generally speaking does swing slightly more than Ether; however, Bitcoin has always been the number one cryptocurrency, carrying out huge brand value with the most developers behind it as well as being the most decentralized project. Unless the currency is up over 10% in the last 24hours, you may invest whenever you wish if you are in it for the long-term.

Famous quote within the Bitcoin community has been: "the best time to buy Bitcoin was yesterday". In the case when either Bitcoin or Ethereum has gone up over 10,20% during the last few days, you may want to wait a little bit for the price to correct downward. Even as a long-term holder it is never recommended to buy around all-time high prices, because doing so you essentially limit your profits more while increasing the risk probability. Other than that, putting money into the other coins means you will have to be ready to research a lot and lose most or even all the value of your investment. High risk, high reward. It should be noted that for the traditional investor even Bitcoin is an extremely volatile asset, meaning it can often go up or down double-digit percentage points due to supply and demand, wealthy investors, news, and speculative nature of cryptocurrencies as of now.

When one "invests" without doing their homework, you could call it gambling or speculation if you aren't sure about why you invested in the first place. That being said, you will surely come across many interesting ideas and revolutionary projects with promising technology and developers behind it. Remember, if it looks like a duck, swims like a duck, and quacks like a duck, then it probably is a duck. In other words, if something is too good to be true, makes sure research the fundamentals before investing.

Scammer's Paradise

"Yo, would you like some free Ethereum? Send me 1 Ether I'll send u 5 back" – Smart scammer

The citation was actually real in case you wonder. Somehow these "first send me 1 & I send you 10 back", are still a thing. If you somehow fall for those types of scams, then there might not be much hope for you. You should also avoid "free" coins, there is no such thing as free coins. More on this later.

This is a double-edged sword. "Trustless" or "decentralized" are both definitely great ideas in theory. However, it brings out the same age-old issue of certain people trying to take advantage over the uninformed. There are of course certain solutions, like regulation, but in a way any form of regulation is of course a bit controversial when we are talking about something with no direct host. Anyway, I have spent a good amount of time trying to figure the definition of a scam. When you think about life in general, it is actually quite hard to draw a clear line on what is and is not a scam. That is, when you really think about it in detail. Surely, we could have a look at the legal definition: Legally, a scam is fraud. Fraud requires (1) false (2) statements (3) that we're made with the intent to deceive, and (4) that the recipient was deceived, who then (5) suffered a loss as a result, but it doesn't provide you with a perfect answer to each individual case. Let us entertain ourselves with some thoughts.

Example A: If you have to take a debt (certain countries), to attend college, but you fail to get concrete value in return (job with the needed skills most likely). Could it be considered a scam? What if they advertise false promises on top of it?

Example B: If someone you truly trust passes you completely false information unknowingly, could they still be considered a scammer?

Example C: If someone deceived with their system but you and the majority greatly profited from it before finding out, while the minority was losing, does this make the deceiving person a fraud?

If there was any point to this, it is the fact that things are never black and white. Since there are over a thousand different cryptocurrencies (most really being scams), there is just no way to look at every single one of them. While some are innocent until proven guilty, one should form educated decision on each case before buying anything. During this book we shall play along with the legal definition. Also, legally Bitcoin is not a scam if that makes you feel any better.

Billy is young ambitious investor. He has made little profits from cryptocurrencies here and there. Now he has found completely new blockchain based lending project promising 0.5-1% daily interest rate on his investment, which will be locked on the platform for certain amount of time. Billy is not too familiar with economics, in fact, he just likes investing because it's quick and simple. Billy decides to invest all of his previous profits into this new lending platform thinking he has made a great long-term investment. Billy soon realizes how much money he could make in only one year. Now he keeps reinvesting more money and the gained interest. Soon Billy finds out the lending platform is offering great bonuses whenever he refers someone else to the platform through his link and even when that someone else refers their friend into the platform Billy gets rewarded! Billy starts promoting the platform and soon he has referred many of his friends and they all started referring their friends. Some of his friends tell him it's not sustainable and surely a scam. Billy doesn't mind, they are just jealous of his success. Two months later, Billy is extremely happy with the results and decides to keep investing more on the platform. Then, two months later, the platform shuts down and Billy and the friends he referred lost all of their money with it. As you can imagine, his friends weren't happy with that.

These type of pyramid scams are quite frequent in the unregulated space of cryptocurrencies. Although most of them die out almost immediately, some keep luring more uninformed victims. Our example story refers to the biggest scam so far, known as "Bitconnect". Technically, one may argue it is not only limited to the tiny projects, but also the "established" ones that will eventually fail. Unfortunately, the scams are getting extremely smart and complicated, meaning they could even last for years. Many of the cryptocurrencies compete with each other directly. You really have to be careful with something you do not fully understand as people may try to influence you. Although Bitcoin is one of the few that is certainly not a scam, you should understand its purpose fully before buying even 0.01 Bitcoin. Same goes to other cryptocurrencies. Each cryptocurrency and blockchain based project has its own strengths and weaknesses, your job is to find them out and decide why you want to be involved with a certain crypto, that is, if you wish to get involved into multiple cryptocurrencies. More on this later, but always consider the long-term sustainability of a coin.

Now I know this sounds like a lot of work, and you just much rather put your money into the next greatest "100x your money now coin", but remember they are always extremely risky. Are you willing to possibly lose all your money in hopes of doubling, tripling, quadrupling the investment? Play accordingly but remember, taking a loss is often hard. If you understand and are willing to take greater risks for greater returns, then you might want to keep an eye on the market and over time you will find some projects with great potential that you really like (that could also bring very significant profits). The market is constantly changing, and if you are interested in multiple coins, you have to follow the market pretty actively so keep that in mind. Above all, be careful, stay safe and do the boring research first. Later on, we will focus more on how to identify the ideal projects with proper due diligence.

Chapter Five: Pros and Cons – The Story of Bitcoin

Due to nature of cryptocurrencies you will find countless of mutable views. It is only human nature to disagree with each other. We shall mainly skip these opinions in this book because this book is specifically for individuals who have little to no previous knowledge on the topic. We are interested in facts. If you were to learn merely one thing out of everything in this book, remember this. Bitcoin is an experiment and like all experiments, it can fail. Don't invest what you can't afford to lose (needless to say the same applies even more on altcoins). Even a chimpanzee would probably agree to not gamble more money than it wanted to lose, but it is not always that simple. *Actually*, the chimpanzee could hit it big as crypto investor. On a side note, I find it rather interesting that the Bitcoin experiment has been one of the first technological outbreaks open for the general public arguably since day one, or at the very least since very early stages.

The story behind Bitcoin

It's time for a little story, recalling back almost ten years. Three individuals, Neal Kin, Vladimir Oksman, and Charles Bry file an application for an encryption patent application. All three individuals deny having any connection to Satoshi Nakamoto. The three also register the site Bitcoin.org in the same month, over on anonymousspeech.com – Site allowing people to buy domain names anonymously.

It is year 2008. Right after one the worst financial crisis, someone with an account called Satoshi Nakamoto published a nine-page white paper containing the first-ever mention of

Bitcoin, calling it a "peer-to-peer electronic cash system." A few months later, Nakamoto released Bitcoin's first software and partnered with developers and coders online to improve it. Bitcoin is valued at $1 = 1.3 BTC. 2010 first Bitcoin market is created, a programmer in Florida buys the famous pizza for 10,000BTC. Later in 2010 Bitcoin gets hacked and goes under the spotlight, leading Bitcoin to be valued at $0.50/BTC. Beginning of 2011, Silk Road (deep web drug market) starts to use Bitcoins as an untraceable way to trade drugs. Leaving the bias of "illegal money".

This collaborative environment continued until 2011 when, without warning, Nakamoto vanished. One Bitcoin worth around 30$. Before ceasing all online communication, they emailed a fellow Bitcoin developer saying they had "moved on to other things." Which happened right after one of their earliest online developers mentioned CIA interview he had been invited to.

Essentially leaving the Bitcoin project and creating one of the only truly decentralized cryptocurrencies. Throughout the years Bitcoin's code has received contributions by hundreds of different individuals. Long story short, anybody can participate by contributing or voting on the Bitcoin core open source. Who has the final say what is eventually implemented or not, is whole another topic, but simplified the new proposals have to receive wide range of consensus by various of different individuals, from miners, wallets, exchanges to the core developers with the final implementation, essentially resulting into slower development process as well as even hard forks, such as Bitcoin cash which forked out of Bitcoin in 2017.

Now back to the story, there was a catch: Nakamoto didn't walk away empty-handed. Sergio Demian Lerner, an Argentine researcher, has estimated that Nakamoto accumulated around a million Bitcoins before disappearing.

Matt Green, a cryptocurrency professor at Johns Hopkins University, says Nakamoto has the power to tank the currency if they want to. Bitcoin has a finite supply of 21 million which is expected to be reached by the year 2140. Nakamoto's one million Bitcoins amount to roughly five percent of the entire cryptocurrency. At the end of 2017, one Bitcoin is valued at over 10,000$

"The thing about Bitcoin is if you control a million of them, you have the ability to flood the market at any point. Think of them as rare baseball cards. They're valuable because they're rare. If somebody could dump hundreds or thousands of Mickey Mantle trading cards, rare ones, onto the market, they wouldn't be worth so much anymore," said Green.

Essentially, if Nakamoto chose to sell their Bitcoin, they could flood the market and cause the price of Bitcoin to tank. Ben Yu, a Bitcoin investor living in San Francisco, says Nakamoto's stake in Bitcoin is extremely significant. This however, is no different from any existing currency.

"If Bitcoin fulfills its role of becoming a global currency, then Satoshi Nakamoto would likely be the richest person in the world and also hold a proportionately higher share of the ultimate supply of Bitcoin than something like the U.S. government holds in gold today," said Yu.

Yu's math works out. The U.S. government holds the most gold reserves of any other entity in the world, at about 8,000 tonnes. That's a little over four percent of the world's total supply, less than Nakamoto's five percent stake in Bitcoin. Some analysts believe Bitcoin's rally is only just beginning. Only one percent of internet users own Bitcoin, and it's valued at over 10,000$.

Kay Van-Petersen, a Saxo Bank analyst, told CNBC in May that he estimates Bitcoin could hit $100,000 by 2025. If that prediction comes true, Nakamoto would have around $100 billion.

This itself, is extremely unlikely risk, but still a possibility. Assuming Bitcoin was to remain the number one cryptocurrency in the future; Some believe it could even replace a dollar, but what would happen when this unknown individual or group of people decided to start purposely flood the market completely? Now it isn't something you want to stress over, just keep it in mind when investing in Bitcoin. Now the same argument can obviously be presented to the dollar as well. This dilemma is very present on other cryptocurrencies, where the foundation claims 10-20% of the entire pre-mined token supply from the get-go. Bitcoin remains as one of the most decentralized currencies ever created.

Now on the later investigation, it's believed that NSA and other institutions, identified the "Nakamoto Mystery" through a method known as stylometry. Which basically is comparing someone's known writings and emails on the internet with trillions of writing samples with every other web user. It's then been suggested with research that "Satoshi Nakamoto" aka. the Bitcoin creator is likely a small group of people. However, the names of these individuals are not out for public, suggesting that the identities may not even be certain, or kept out on purpose. Anyhow, the mystery of Satoshi Nakamoto continues.

The true beauty behind the mystery is the art like symbolism behind Satoshi. We still have no idea who really created Bitcoin. All the hints behind the character clearly point against the way of traditional currency. Bitcoin was released right after the 2008 economic crash. Satoshi's birthday was chosen as the day when US federal reserve confiscated all the gold from its citizens (this couldn't be executed to Bitcoin in the same manner). On top of this, Satoshi never chose to sell any of their early mined Bitcoins as of late. The dollar value for Satoshi's Bitcoins range between multiple billions ever since middle 2017. This may cause concern, not knowing the creator but is it really needed? Personally, the symbolism of Satoshi reminds me of "Batman begins" (2005 funnily enough) , just because in a way the message of Satoshi could suggest that everyone can be Satoshi. Well, at least it is close enough for a real life example, right...? Essentially, anybody can go out there, learn about bitcoin, contribute to Bitcoin code, mine it, buy or sell bitcoin, and share the idea. There is no one direct entity as in traditional manner. Of course, in real life this pitch perfect utopian currency is not quite the same but it certainly has benefits over the current monetary system.

Bitcoin has had an incredible journey to this day, going far back over 15-years from the initial idea of e-gold as internet gold, different political views, all the way from vision for change to the release of Bitcoin and its growth and struggle of being owned by only developers and criminals. Bitcoin may never replace current financial systems like united states dollar but even if it somehow did, we'd probably be living in vastly different societies from today. Bitcoin could very well remain as the "digital gold" though. Are you excited enough to get through some bullet point listings? Let's dedicate it for Satoshi.

Downsides and risks:

These points apply, generally speaking, to all cryptocurrencies. Many of the more recent projects have more and more solutions to the current problems of Bitcoin & Ethereum, but in return sacrifice other important aspects such as decentralization as they are basically run like regular companies. We can't really say which risk applies specifically to an "X" crypto in this brief generic listing, but the very basic idea is similar, and you can later read the ideas behind each currency to make your own decision how good or bad it is. One of the easiest ways to get basic understanding of a specific cryptocurrency is to simply visit their website. As we speak right now, Bitcoin is still the safest cryptocurrency in terms of probability. We shall talk more on identifying the quality projects later.

- **Lack of Knowledge** and therefore a high level of entry. Okay so an older person just got their first computer, started reading news online and now there's internet money? Not only money, but everything is moving into completely new and different technology. Imagine the reaction. This technology can be really hard to understand for many people. How long will it take for the majority to fully accept the concept? The Internet has slowly begun to take place for all ages over the past 10 years. Even though it was presented to the public around another 10 years ago. Technology and the interface aren't beginner friendly at the moment either. Which in general means less acceptance. However, in theory, this could also be positive since you reading this book could take advantage of the situation as an early adopter - depending on when you're reading of course. In other words, complicated user interface for now.

- **No Specific Regulations:** This is slowly starting to change a little bit as I'm writing this book. By the end of 2017, it's announced that Bitcoin futures will be available December 18th. US exchanges CBOE and CME are the ones offering those contracts at the moment. On top of this, many of the biggest crypto platforms are regulated. However, this doesn't apply to all countries or platforms. Then again, the scene has slowly gained regulation from the beginning. One the big arguments to regulate cryptocurrencies has been based on the illegal transactions made in cryptocurrencies. However, for now criminal acts with cryptocurrency is a non-argument. The vast majority of crime is done with USD.

- **Uncertainty:** We already established this is new technology. This means the uncertainty and speculation around cryptocurrency will remain for upcoming years, which adds extra fear. Since in the absolutely worst case you could either; 1. Lose most of your money 2. Lose ALL of your money. On top of this, as the technology is new and developing, mistakes are inevitable and we can't guarantee anything.

- **Recovery:** Unlike banks that can cover you in case of a security issue like a hack or stolen credit card, cryptocurrency isn't retrievable when lost. As we mentioned previously, there are recovery methods under development. Again, uncertainty and new technology.

- **Mining:** Few biggest miners have relatively high control over Bitcoin, and this is only going to increase as the mining gets more difficult. Different mining formats have their weaknesses.

  - **Scalability:** how practical is Bitcoin going to be? Recently, with all the increasing adoptions, it seems Bitcoin can't handle mass use very well. Transactions are slower, fees are getting higher, and many rush in for the "quick money" without understanding the concept. On top of this, how practical do you think the 21million supply? (Lower than 21million in practice) Does it seem reasonable to play around with satoshis (0.00000001 BTC). Or will Bitcoin remain more as an investment while new cryptocurrency project will take over as an actual currency?

  - **Banks:** cryptocurrencies being direct competition to traditional banking systems, many banks have started to take major action against cryptocurrencies and some have even gone as far as refusing to receive any money that is sent from a cryptocurrency exchange. This makes it a lot more difficult to move money in and out. Email vs. mail.

- **Government and cryptocurrency:** At which point do governments get involved? (China's Bitcoin ban) The principles of cryptocurrency mean they couldn't track, control, or tax this currency. One reason why it's completely starting to blow off in many countries right now. They couldn't snoop into our bank accounts whenever they wanted to. Again, taxing these currencies is more complicated. More regulations are constantly being pushed into cryptocurrencies. Basically, they wouldn't be in as much control. Do you really think that will happen? Sounds pretty interesting though, even appealing, doesn't it? What type of regulations will take place and how will affect the market? Feel free to discuss all the new secret Bitcoin government theories on the internet. Yes, you can find... well, rather interesting claims.

- **Centralization:** One significant problem lies on the "fake decentralized" cryptocurrencies. What I mean by this is there are many cryptocurrencies where considerable amount of the circulating coin supply is held by the creators and developers. Creating highly centralized environment and power distribution. Whereas Satoshi has at most approximately 5% of the Bitcoins, divided by possibly more than one person, most of the altcoin teams hold 10-30% of the total supply as reserve. Which brings out the argument that many altcoins are merely a scam. Making Bitcoin the most decentralized cryptocurrency at the moment. Specific distribution information on each project can be found on their respective websites. However, one could argue there is no such thing as true decentralization, Bitcoin definitely comes close (in theory), but are not absolute in reality.

- **Manipulation**: It is easy for big players to manipulate the markets. It has been blatant obvious since the launch of the CME futures in Dec. of 2017. Whether or not one perceives manipulation as negative or positive is up to them. Of course, traditional markets are manipulated as well at a lot smaller scale but unregulated cryptocurrencies are very heavily controlled. Another reason to not invest more than you would practically gamble. More on actual ideas and tips for the market later but this way you will maximize the chances of actually taking profits when it is due (i.e. the price valuations are way over the top like December 2017). Think of it like a casino where the probabilities are in your favor.

Bitcoin being the biggest crypto, it gets often over pumped due to mass ignorance as well as constant back and forth transactions between BTC – altcoins, leading to huge price fluctuation, although it is the biggest cryptocurrency. This isn't necessarily bad thing for a trader or long-term investor. Bitcoin is often regarded as the "blockchain 1.0" in terms of its technology against some of the other projects. These projects do not directly compete with Bitcoin though since they are not developed to act as payment currency. It should be noted that Bitcoin has by no doubt the biggest brand out there. Having the brand has its own underlying value, but this also means high volatility. While the market of Bitcoin keeps on growing, the supply and demand without specific regulations combined with a lot of speculative investors has made Bitcoin extremely volatile for its size. Many are blindly shouting "take my life savings" in hopes of quick money without any understanding of its features, often resulting into panic selling when the market is going down, this dilemma has followed rather similarly on the altcoins. It has always worked out in the end so far, but will it go on forever?

The biggest argument against Bitcoin or any cryptocurrency for that matter, is volatility. How can we ever use something so volatile as a global currency? It's a great argument indeed and many consider Bitcoin as the digital version of gold's "store of value". There are many risk factors with cryptocurrencies, why would you even want to consider being involved yet? Next, we are going to take a look at the benefits cryptocurrencies offer.

Remember, if the technology is truly revolutionary and life changing, it will always exist the same way that the dollar has existed despite the numerous wars, bloodshed, crimes, evil, laundering, and suffering that has been perpetuated at its hands.

> *"The longer the bull market lasts, the more severely investors will be affected with amnesia. After five years or so, many people no longer believe that bear markets are possible."*
> – Benjamin Graham, The Intelligent Investor

Pros:

- **Fraud-Proof:** Digital currency, specifically Bitcoin is technology wise safer than "real" paper currency. It has zero chance of being a fraud in itself. As you already know, they operate under the blockchain technology, that is essentially decentralized global ledger of every single transaction. Giving you proper privacy and control. The only issue here is human psychology, do we perceive it as something valuable?

- **Stealing Identity:** Not possible. User has control to send only the designated amount with no additional information. Also, you can diversify your storages, more on this in chapter 11.

- **Low fees:** digital currency itself has extremely low transaction fees. The amount of fee you pay generally varies around cents. However, many exchange platforms charge fees. These fees are still relatively low, as long as you minimize unnecessary transactions between exchanges.

- **Processing:** Blockchain enables smart contracts, which meant no third-party approval needed. Which means way faster processing on transactions. Varying from few seconds to minutes.

- **Power to the people!** Okay, that was a pretty revolutionary title I admit. Cryptocurrencies are more decentralized than the current system giving the access to everyone. You could, for example, buy an item from a website that accepts Bitcoins using your digital Bitcoin wallet, just you and the provider in essence. This could include many people who do not have online access to regular payment methods ("X" countries). Basically, whether you are a president or 16-year old blogger, you are equal to everyone else in the blockchain. Nobody can take your Bitcoin, you are in control.

- **Massive investment returns (potentially):** I Probably don't need to explain more. Remember Bitcoin's price back in 2015, Ethereum, Litecoin, Dash... the list goes on and on. It is a speculative asset.

- **Inflation is extremely unlikely:** As you know traditional currency experiences small yearly inflation because economies shift prices and governments keep printing more money. Bitcoin – 21 million coins to ever be mined, which can't be altered. Ever.

- **This makes the US Dollar value to crypto go up by default:** As long as there is demand for any cryptocurrency, its price keeps going higher in fiat money because all the major cryptocurrencies; Bitcoin, Litecoin, Ethereum or even high supply currencies like Cardano are deflating with the amount they will be mined, eventually reaching the total supply. For instance, 21million Bitcoins. While governments keep printing more and more regular fiat money each year causing inflation by default.

- **Revolutionizing the way we have viewed technology:** Technology is evolving faster than ever before. Blockchain, along with artificial intelligence is arguably one of the biggest technological revolutions ever since the creation of internet, causing radical changes for many industries in the near future. This will unfortunately include changes in many of the current jobs and professions.

"Without the need to trust a third-party middleman, money can be secure and transactions effortless."

– Satoshi Nakamoto, developer(s) of Bitcoin

During its brief history, Bitcoin has proved to greatly appreciate against the USD (deflationary). Bitcoin has a lot of arguments for and against it. However, one the biggest arguments against Bitcoin being a valid currency, is the lack of stability in its price. Why would anybody want to pay with Bitcoin today, if it could be up 50% the next year? Again, there are arguments on both sides here, but one of the most likely scenarios revolves around Bitcoin ending up as the digital store of value. Hence the nickname "digital gold". Cryptocurrencies may not be perfect but let us not forget that the banking system is far from perfect as well (some may call it corrupted). In the next chapter, we are going to get back to history class as we will take a brief look at the development of money throughout the evolution of human civilization.

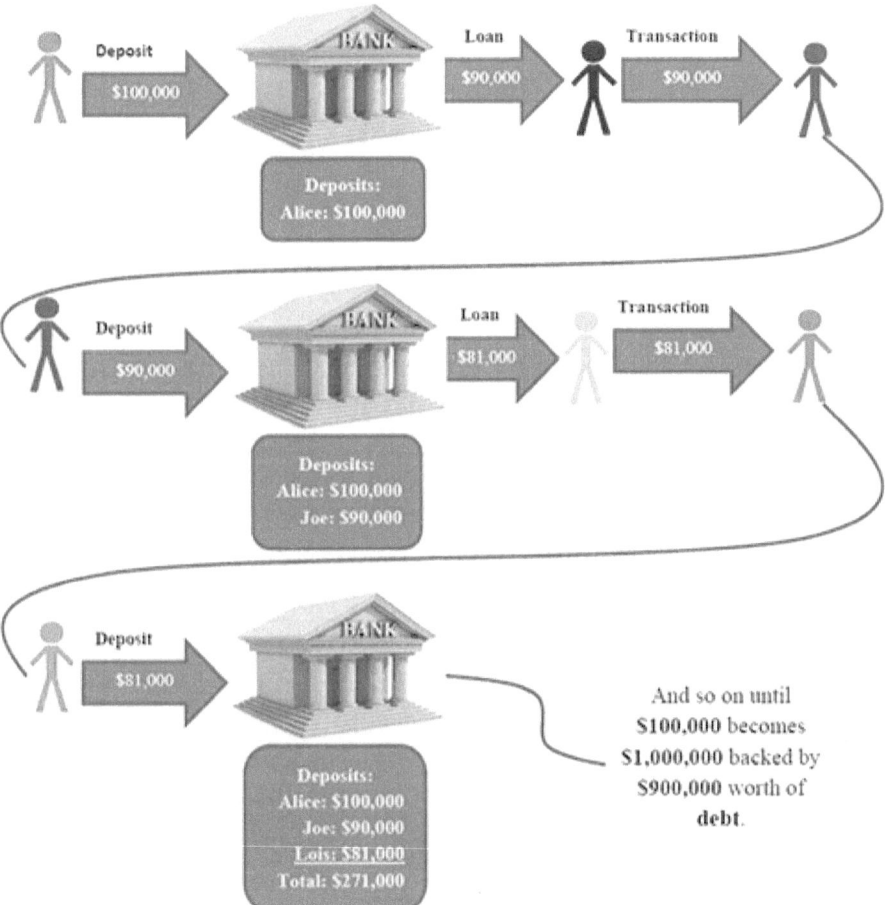

In short, banks create the money in the course of making loans, which means they can charge interest on money they create at essentially no cost to themselves. If enough people decided to withdraw their deposits out of the bank account at the same time, the bank would not be able to pay them.

Chapter Six: Development of Money – Resisting Change

"Change or Die"

People often resist the change and therefore get stuck in the old and outdated. I think we all know at least that one person who is still bashing on smartphones in 2017, or whatever the specific change they resist is. The thing is, once we get to understand something, it becomes comfortable and part of our subconscious self-image. Those aware are generally speaking open to changes because they know it's the essence of life.

However, you shouldn't look to change just for the sake of it. You should look for change IF, it brings a new solution or something really valuable. For instance, let's say you start to eat healthier and exercise. In the beginning, it's hard, and you are overwhelmed. However, after few months of the process you start to slowly see the difference. Eating healthy and exercising has become a habit to you. You are starting to see the value it brings to your life. Now it would be hard to suddenly quit this habit again.

The thing with habits is that our brain is wired to look for habits and once you have established one, even a bad habit, it's hard to replace this habit because on average it takes 30 to 90 days for a new habit to take place. The more complicated the habit is to establish, the longer it takes to form.

Common psychological reaction to change.

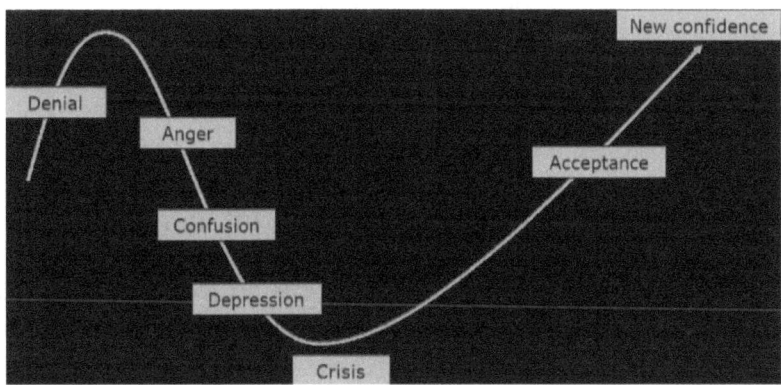

Evolution of Money

Billy asks his parents: "Where does all the money come from?"

"Government makes it through banks."

Billy: "how?"

"They print it."

Billy: "why can't I have more money then?"

Do we really even understand how money works? Over time we've created different forms of abstractions with different technologies. Money itself is just an abstraction. Giving fruits in exchange for wood is barter. Changing one commodity for another. Abstract however, doesn't have any practical use in itself. It represents shared value, shared delusion. This shared value comes from the assumption that I can use this money again.

With cryptocurrency, many believe it's not real money (fake internet money not backed by anything!!). However, funnily enough, it was the same story when metal coins were introduced as a form of money. Why is money money? It's because we think it's money. You can live on Bitcoin, you can sell Bitcoin, you could have become a millionaire with Bitcoin. Is it money? Why is the US dollar money? The dollar hasn't been backed by gold for decades, governments are free to print more of it (if you don't believe me, which you shouldn't you can see it for yourself). Why is it more of a money than Bitcoin? Because more people believe it's more of a money than Bitcoin. Bitcoin for the average user, like your bank account, is merely a series of numbers on a screen. The difference here is that Bitcoin is actually mathematically backed up. Basically, gold is backed by faith that alchemy doesn't work. Bitcoin is backed by faith that math does work (more specifically, cryptographic primitives which Bitcoin uses won't be broken, i.e. that mathematicians won't find a computationally cheap way to reverse ECDSA and SHA256 computations / faith that people will keep choosing Bitcoin over some other cryptocurrency.), while dollars are backed by faith that governments always pay their debts.

Money, as we know it today, is the result of a very long process. To understand money today, it's important to know its evolution throughout history. In the beginning, there was no money in the concept we now use it. Everything was connected in barter, the exchange of merchandise for merchandise, without any specific equivalence. But it doesn't mean we didn't have "money."

What is the definition of money itself? Here are some common definitions you can find:

"Money is any clearly identifiable object of value that is generally accepted as payment for goods and services and repayment of debts within a market or which is legal tender within a country" – Wikipedia.org

"Current medium of exchange in the form of coins and banknotes; coins and banknotes collectively" – Google search definition

"Something generally accepted as a medium of exchange, a measure of value, or a means of payment" – Webster dictionary

Prehistory, primitive money

Animals, fruits, and vegetables were being used as a common medium of exchange in the primitive hunting stage. History records that cattle occupied a place of pride as money in the primitive human civilization. Everyone had to know their debts, since there was no ledger to track who owned what.

In temperate regions of Europe, Asia, and Africa cattle was regarded as the most standard unit of barter for quite a long time in the primitive era. In the ancient Indian civilization, the concept of cattle wealth as a form of money is also referred to in Arth-Veda. In the fourth century B.C., the Roman State had officially recognized cows and sheep as money to collect fines and taxes.

The Greek philosopher Aristotle contemplated the nature of money. He considered that every object has two uses, the first being the original purpose for which the object was designed, and the second possibility to conceive the object as an item to sell and barter.

Commodity Money

Slowly different communities started to use certain items as default commodity money. This was dependent upon various factors such as: location of the community, environment and economic standards, etc.

For example, people living near seas adopted different shells and dried fishes as a form of money. Cold regions like Alaska and Siberia started to use skins and furs as money.

Then there were more developed agriculture civilizations like the Mesopotamia and later Babylonia starting to scale the system with silver, bronze, copper, etc.

Metallic Money

While basic materials such as grain and wood were popular commodity in the early stages of ancient Greece and Mediterranean Sea, the use of metal as currency started to take its place. As soon as more and more communities discovered metal, it was used for various purposes like weapons, tools, and utensils. Quickly metal also became the main standard of value. Usage of metals as a form of money led to the development of coins. Coins in ancient Greece were born with weight measurement and labeling.

Then the Roman Empire started using silver coins as the common money, which at the time was closest to fiat currency we now have. Some regions even outside of the Roman empire's bounds accepted the Roman silver coins as their currency. Eventually, the great Roman empire disintegrated and so did the value of the silver coin. Massive inflation as we know it today. As the empire deteriorated more and more, basic commodity money took the front seat again. Wine and grain were popular means of payment again.

Throughout the development of Middle Ages in Europe the economy started slowly recovering from agriculture back to coins.

Early Paper Money

This Greek story was a popular one amongst the lands of ancient Silk Road. What is the moral of the story?

Once upon a time, there was a man who owned a wonderful goose. Every morning, this goose laid for him a beautiful egg – not an ordinary egg, an egg made of pure shiny solid gold. Every morning, the man collected a new golden egg. And day by day, egg by egg, the man began to grow rich. But he started to want more. "My goose has all those golden eggs inside her" he kept thinking. "Why not get them all at once? I want fortunes now! I don't want to wait years to get rich" Then, one day he just couldn't wait any longer. He grabbed the goose and killed her. But there were no eggs inside her. As the man cried, he asked: "Why did I do that? Now there will be no more eggs." Eventually, the man lost all the eggs he once had and died poor.

While Europe was recovering, the Middle East and Asia had active trading. Silk road was born. Silk road was used to transport many different merchandises like; gold, gemstones, coins, and silk. Along with the merchandised exchange, Silk road has had a big impact on the overall culture and development of money. It could be viewed as one of the first bigger "global" markets at the time. Not quite the global as we know, but global for its time period. In the 17th and 18th centuries, early paper currency started to emerge. Originally it appeared as paper receipts against metallic money which was found unsafe to carry as a merchant.

Then as the economy thrived, shortage of metals lead to the introduction of paper currency. Later, as paper money developed, it basically became fiat money i.e., money we know today.

Bank Money and Monetary Systems

Finally, banks and government started to emerge. Different countries developed their monetary systems. People started to use banks. Even checks were a form of dematerialized money. Later, as you know, we started using credit cards and digital payment services like PayPal. During more recent history, things like cigarettes and cognac were used as money during World War 2. Basically, anything and everything can serve and HAS served as money throughout history. As we stated at the beginning of this chapter. Money is simply something that can provide value.

Are cryptocurrencies the next form of money?
PS: looking to trade 31 pearls, 15 sea shells, a chicken and 5 euros for 0.014 Bitcoins.

Chapter Seven: Digital Currency in 2020 - The Future of Money?

"Cryptocurrencies will be worth more than FOUR trillion US$ by 2020. Like the "eternal" September in 1993, this June 2017 will be remembered as the "Ethernal June" (a term I just invented now), the month in which pretty much the world started to hear about Ethereum (and ICOs), and pay much closer attention to Bitcoin."

Vitalik Buterin, the young co-founder of Ethereum platform:

"Currently (June, 2017), the "market cap" of all cryptocurrencies is at about $110 Billions, of which $43B is Bitcoin, and $37B is Ethereum. For the first time since Bitcoin's inception, it is very clear that cryptocurrencies are here to stay. Their critical mass, their momentum, the investments being made, and finally, a huge interest from governments (including Vladimir Putin, quite surprisingly) mean that in the next *two-three* years so many valuable things will be built on top of this technology, and that Bitcoin (or Ethereum) has the chance to become the world's first truly global currency, independent from any specific country or corporation."

Well, maybe not quite so fast. The fantasy of 'de-politicized,' 'honest' money may be just too good to be true. Political aspects aside, there's no denying that cryptocurrencies are going to become a fundamental part of our daily lives in near future. Their ability to be programmed and updated allowed them to grow from just an insanely complicated tool to buy two pizzas to a monetary juggernaut that every financial institution is now dealing with, including Goldman Sachs.

Goldman Sachs' coverage of Bitcoin:

Goldman believes cryptocurrencies value will be four trillion US$ by 2020, which is about 40x value of the day they gave the coverage.

"If people keep believing in cryptocurrencies as a store of value / a good investment / whatever, then its potential as an asset has barely started to build up. It is not hard to imagine that it could capture a value in the same ballpark as gold's assets, which are worth $8.2 Trillion today."

It is also not too hard to imagine that if the market cap grew about 40x from November 2013 ($3.3B) to July 2017, it might as well grow another 40x or so in the next 3.5 years (end of 2020). Unfortunately, there is really no other data point that we can reliably use.

Goldman Sachs mentions a few things that could happen, and could justify this 40x jump:

- "An X cryptocurrency to measure, and exchange, reputation among humans."

- "An X cryptocurrency to invest in any artist (musicians, painters) and gain returns if the artist in which you invested is successful."

- "An X cryptocurrency that will seriously challenge our current Cloud providers (AWS, Azure, Google Compute Platform) by offering compute, storage and higher-level services without the limitations or impositions of a central authority (corporation)." Ethereum?

(quotations from medium.com 2020 predictions at 2017 by Vitalik Buterin & Goldman Sachs) 18.11.2017

Now we could go on and on about the cryptocurrency speculation by other "recognized" authorities, as it's still a highly future based concept starting to prove its ground. This asset class is highly speculative and obviously those involved are always going to be at least somewhat biased. However, I'm just trying to give you some basic point of view here.

Nobody knows for certain. You can't predict the future. Don't trust anyone making precise predictions on specific coins. The vast majority of actual experts in and outside of the field are "bullish" on the future of cryptocurrencies and blockchain. We already went through all the major risk points, I added this chapter to give you the speculative side of things to keep in mind. After all, PayPal gained traction because the conventional financial networks of the day weren't meeting all needs. Bitcoin's open architecture could allow it to be even more disruptive. Meaning there could be at least a substantial market for Bitcoin-, crypto-based services on blockchain that perform certain services better. Then again, asking for the opinion of a bank manager might give you a bit different response versus asking someone that is involved with cryptocurrencies. Always aim to keep a realistic point of view.

Especially now that the bigger institutional money is considering getting into Bitcoin. For example, Nasdaq is planning Bitcoin futures in the first half of 2018 and two huge US exchanges that are already launching their Bitcoin futures by the end of 2017, CBOE and CME. If you aren't familiar with traditional investing like stocks for instance, just focus on learning the basics of every asset class first.

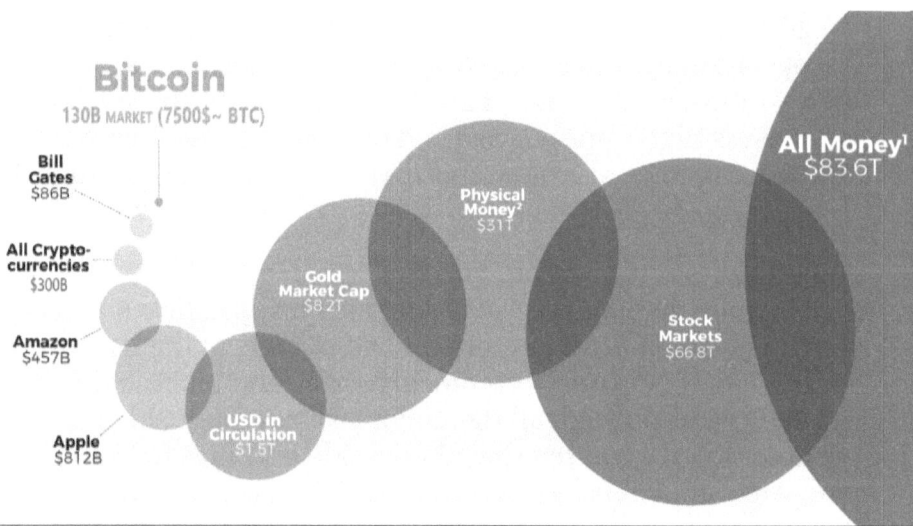

The exact market cap of cryptocurrencies is hard to determine due to many different variables but market cap of 100 billion dollars does not mean there is 100 billion dollars in Bitcoin. Take this picture with a grain of salt. As of now cryptocurrencies are just a tiny part of the whole global finance. $130 billion market cap for Bitcoin equals around seven to eight thousand dollars a coin. Even during Bitcoin's highest peak of $20 000 per coin, its total market cap was below Amazon's (roughly $ 330billion at the all-time high). For perspective, the dotcom bubble was about $3 trillion before bursting, although the definition of a bubble varies a lot.

What do you think the future cities, those ruled by blockchain or artificial intelligence, would look like?

(The Future Site of Wuhan Science and Technology Museum in Wuhan, China)

Chapter Eight: Practicality, the Digital Present

At this point you have hopefully formed a basic picture around Blockchain, Bitcoin, its technology, features, and cryptocurrency in general. If not, you may want to consider a quick recap of the earlier chapters. Now you are wondering "what is the practical use of a cryptocurrency such as Bitcoin?" What can you do right now other than speculate and invest? We will look at what you can buy with Bitcoin, because it's the most accepted coin as of now, while Ethereum being more of an infrastructure than pure currency. However, it is still worth to note that Ethereum blockchain is being used for various different purposes. One of the most recent being Canadian government exploring with the Ethereum blockchain. That being said, you can expect more innovating currencies to be implemented in the future other than just Bitcoin. Some could technically even outperform Bitcoin some day. But enough of the speculation, let's take a look at what you can buy with Bitcoin.

Throughout the past years, countless of different merchants have opened up for Bitcoin. Some billion-dollar companies and some tiny little online shops.

Here's list of the most known companies currently accepting Bitcoins:

- Subway – Certain Subway stores accept Bitcoin
- Microsoft – Users can buy content with Bitcoin on Xbox and Windows store
- Reddit – You can buy premium features with bitcoins

- WordPress.com – An online company
- OkCupid – Online dating site
- CheapAir.com – Travel booking site for airline tickets, car rentals, hotels
- Gyft – Buy gift cards with Bitcoin
- Wikipedia – Added Bitcoin to its donation options
- Bitcoin. Travel – a travel site that provides accommodation, apartments, attractions, bars, and beauty salons around the world
- 4Chan.org – Premium services
- Whole Foods – Organic food store (by purchasing gift card from Gyft)
- Bitcoincoffee.com – Buying coffee online
- Square – Payment processor helping small businesses to accept credit cards using phones.
- Shopify.com – An online store that allows anyone to sell their products
- Famsa – Mexico's biggest retailer
- Rakutan – A Japanese e-commerce giant
- Stripe – San Francisco-based payments company
- Save the Children – Global charity

… and many more!

(list- https://99bitcoins.com/who-accepts-bitcoins-payment-companies-stores-take-bitcoins/ 29.11.2017)

For complete visual representation of Bitcoin merchants around the world. Go to www.coinmap.org.

It's expected that many more companies would start to accept Bitcoin and other cryptocurrencies throughout the year of 2018. For instance, the speculation of when Amazon will start to accept Bitcoin has been around for a while now. Obviously, whenever a bigger company starts to accept Bitcoin, it causes the price of Bitcoin to instantly spike, at least shortly. Generally, there is news whenever a recognized company jumps in, pumping the price up. In the beginning, you will be better off with just investing in an "X" coin and focusing on learning everything you can about the topic, but it's good to keep in mind that more and more companies are starting to see cryptocurrencies. Lately, people have even been selling commodities such as luxury houses and Lamborghinis for Bitcoins.

Or… you could just move to Japan.

In the summer of 2017, over 260 000 stores in total were accepting Bitcoin as payment in Japan, and it's been growing ever since. These shops are able to take the payments with an app called recruit lifestyle. Regular customers can scan a code on the app to pay with their digital currency. There is a lot of different ideas on how the payments will be made in future, but it's a quite interesting idea that in Japan you could **technically** already live on Bitcoins.

In reality though, current Bitcoin fees are unreasonable for the buyer (on the everyday purchases) and even Bitcoin is still mainly considered a capital asset (first fully digital), and long-term investment or form of a trading asset. Also, it makes sense for businesses to accept cryptocurrencies, but if you as a buyer were to make a purchase with Bitcoin, you'd have to also consider the price fluctuation. Due to the nature of cryptocurrencies, they are hardly stable relative to dollar. For instance, does it really make sense for you to pay with Bitcoin if you believe that the value of Bitcoin will rise? Even if the currency experiences mainstream adoption, this dilemma will likely remain for years to come, or forever, which may suggest that the blockchain technology used for regular currency purposes may not happen. It does not necessarily take anything away from other possibilities to carry out sooner though.

Bitcoins in Japan:

Burger King in Arnhem, Netherlands. City known for its Bitcoin acceptance.

Particular Subways have been accepting Bitcoin for years. Lately even Litecoin has been added to few Subway stores.

Same issue remains with other blockchain projects. They are not finished products; therefore, the practical use cases are rather low for the time being. The benefits of blockchain are yet to be realized for the average users. Very similar conditions to the early times of the internet. Next, you will learn some basic investment principles and all the practical aspects of cryptocurrencies in order to maximize the profits, that is, if you wish to get involved with cryptocurrencies.

Chapter Nine: Long-Term Cryptocurrency assets

Before we get started here. I would like to clarify that buying and holding Bitcoin or other cryptocurrencies does not make you an investor. For now, you are a coin/token holder. Not an investor by definition. Although I will keep referring to coin holders as investors. I do this only because it is more practical but it is important to realize the difference between traditional investing and holding cryptocurrency assets.

From an investor's perspective, you could think of all the different cryptocurrencies as individual stocks, all operating on the blockchain technology. Based on which coin(s) you decide to make up your crypto portfolio, you could estimate whether it's more like a steady growth or really high risk, high reward. Of course, we can't compare them directly, but what I'm basically saying is: don't invest all your portfolio into one stock!

Millions of people invest in Bitcoin and other cryptocurrencies. Some are in it for the long-haul, others just to make a quick profit. Many of them end up burning out due to lack of knowledge. Cryptocurrencies have proven to be worth noting. Even for the traditional investors. Yet there are millions of others who don't know how to get involved in trading or where to begin. This chapter covers some of the better ideas, tips and tricks to maximize your cryptocurrency profits, although you must not take this as professional financial advice – these points should give you tremendous help and save you a lot of money and errors. For the most part these tips are timeless, meaning no matter when you are reading this, they still apply just as much, because they are based on human psychology.

Consider how you can use this advice to fit your personal plan. Majority may wish to be a passive / defensive investor although in cryptocurrencies it is not quite the same as traditionally. For example, buying small amount of Bitcoin and leaving the seed to grow. You may wet the seed later as you get to understand it better to grow further but most of the time you just let it be. This requires almost no maintenance and basic knowledge is more than enough. Years later, you may find your seed has grown into a small tree! Someone with more experience may find some of the following tips rather obvious, but it is always worthwhile recapping the basics. Know this. Cryptocurrencies are speculative asset class. Do not use it as means to an end. They should be used as a small portion of your total assets. Investing in cryptocurrencies or Bitcoin is a great tool for additional "passive" income but once you overdo it, problems will arise. I can't stress this enough. Do not repeat the same mistake as millions of others.

- **Don't use a broker;** use a cryptocurrency exchange instead, and you will save on the fees. All the listed exchanges in this book are specific crypto exchanges.
- **Use limit orders** when you use an exchange to buy and sell because they are usually the cheapest for fees. More on limit orders later.
- **Supply and demand** determines the market prices. Multiple external factors affect the balance of supply and demand. In practice, the current circulating supply of Bitcoin is almost 17 million Bitcoins. Out of these 17 million, Satoshi wallets own approximately million coins. According to most studies, 2-4 million Bitcoins are out of circulation due to lost keys, hacks, etc. during the early years of Bitcoin. Then there are the long-term holders, early investors, exchanges, making up several million coins, these coins are out of the current supply since the owners do not wish to sell their coins any time soon. Leaving the realistic market supply on a given day to merely few millions at best. There is obviously a lot more that goes into the exact count, but this is essentially what allows the cryptocurrency prices to swing so radically.
- **Use dollar cost averaging** if you opt to go long. This helps you to avoid making badly timed trades. Dollar cost averaging merely means to buy in increments on regular a schedule rather than all at the same time. Helps you to keep emotions detached from your investments. Recommended strategy especially for beginners.
- **Common sense – buy low and sell high.** Watch the trends in price; if you are looking at the highest price in the last 24 hours, then that's a risky time to invest. Watch for when the price breaks out but exercise caution

- **Don't put all your eggs into one basket.** If you do, you won't be able to buy another currency when it hits a dip. So, keep some money back for those eventualities. If you are all in with one currency, you will have a harder time holding it if the price goes down. Consider to diversify if your position is getting too itchy bur remember this could also sign that you are over invested in cryptocurrencies!
- **Bitcoin is king, or is it?** Yes, no, just kidding yes! (maybe…) Don't get too enthusiastic about the other coins as a beginner. Be extremely cautious on the projects that are trying directly to replace Bitcoin. i.e. cryptocurrencies whom main goal is to function as a currency. If you already invested in Bitcoin and the price stands still and other coins look to be increasing in value, don't get itchy fingers. Also, keep in mind that the majority knows only Bitcoin and therefore blindly invests in it. Bitcoin is needed to buy many altcoins and ultimately the brand "Bitcoin" is more valuable than you might think
- **Keep in mind that Bitcoin and Altcoins sometimes do the same** and at other times they do the opposite of one another. It is not unheard of for Bitcoin to go up and Altcoins to go down or vice versa and this is because those who invest in both will move out of Bitcoin when the price drops and go into the Altcoins. However, sometimes both will go up or down at the same time. Generally speaking, altcoin prices are rather dependent on Bitcoin's price
- **Diversify.** Keeping that in mind, don't lose control and move into, say, ETH when BTC fails and risk missing out on a spike in the price and then shifting back to BTC and

missing the spike in ETH. Diversify and invest in several different coins. That way you will avoid the chance of missing a unicorn – this is a rare or strange event, like a huge spike in price in a short space of time. However, remember to hold the majority of your investments around the top 5 coins, and specifically on Bitcoin, unless you prefer higher risk.

- **Total portfolio diversity.** Unless you consider the invested sum to be insignificantly small, it is worthwhile diversifying between different asset classes, not only cryptocurrencies but stocks, funds, bonds, etc. This becomes even more important when you realize significant profits from your existing cryptocurrency assets, and when you are either reinvesting or pushing new money into cryptocurrencies. The percentage points of which you should divide your total portfolio between different assets classes should be decided based on your individual investment strategy, and current conditions.
- **Start out slow.** Unless you have previous experience on investing, build your portfolio slowly but surely. Many studies have suggested that losses are as impactful, psychologically, as gains, known as loss aversion. Loss aversion implies that one who loses 100$ will lose more satisfaction than another person will gain from a 100$ profit. Taking losses may scare many new investors out of the market. I would also highly recommend learning about traditional assets.
- **Aggressive vs. defensive plan.** Someone with extremely aggressive strategy might split even up to 20% of their total portfolio assets into cryptocurrencies, while a defensive plan may be looking cryptocurrency investments as low as 1-5% of the portfolio's total value.

- **Diversity will cost you.** Having a diverse investment strategy and portfolio is likely to cost you a bit in gains as well as keeping losses to a minimum. If you really want to make huge profits all the time, then you must be prepared to make some rather **risky** trades. Go all in on a single coin and the price shoots up, but if it drops, your funds are all locked into that currency while you wait for the price to rise again. While a diverse strategy will provide a certain amount of protection and ease of mind, it will also reduce your gains as it is highly unlikely for everything to go up or down. Base your diversity on what you think will fit best to your specific conditions.
- **Hold, range, dip and set orders.** By this, I mean that you should hold some coins, range trade on others, keep some coins back for dips and set both high and low-ball orders. This will make sure that, no matter what happens, you are set up for what happens next. It can be very tempting to either go all in on one or cash out altogether, but disappointment will only set in when the market does the opposite.
- **Stick with your strategy.** On some occasions, the market is going to be a little crazy and it might make sense to sell or buy, but don't change your entire strategy until you have given it some serious thought.
- **Beware of scams.** There are a lot of them, and I mean **a lot**. Be extremely critical when taking advice regarding specific cryptocurrency, most of the time you will get biased opinion, (basically someone being overly positive on a coin they own) and if you can't find anything good about a coin, then it most likely has some sort of scam attached to it. Example on previous mass-marketing scams: Bitconnect cryptocurrency lending platform & all

its promoters. These may be difficult to identify at first, which is why you have to choose how much time you are willing to spend researching a specific coin.
- **Beware of market manipulation and spoofers.** Spoofing is what caused the flash crash of the stock market in 2010 and, in cryptocurrency, the crash is 10 times worse. If a price spike or drop seems to be too good to be true, then it is most likely the work of a manipulator. This is quite a common occasion in the crypto markets due to the fear of missing out on something big.
- **Common sense – don't invest more money than you can afford to lose.** Probably mentioned this couple of times at this point…There really isn't anything else to say here, it is common sense. Many think they know how much money they can afford to lose in theory, but in reality, they often end up panic selling the market correction.
- **Take your profits.** Some investors think this is the wrong thing to do but it is more of a conservative type of strategy. Yes, you may make less money in the long-run than if you had just left your money but that will only be true if your choice of investments rises in price. Taking decent profits and then waiting until the price drops again is a better strategy. This way you minimize the emotional attachment to your investments as you are only playing with accumulated profits. i.e. you invest 100$ and your investment multiplied enough that you can take your 100$ out and still hold significant amount of coins.
- **Set your limit orders for a bit over or under the recent lows and highs.** This will result in your

cryptocurrency being sold before it hits a resistance point, meaning you are more likely to make a profit. Not available in Coinbase, move to GDAX later if you start with Coinbase. (next chapter)

- **Bitcoin resistance tends to be whole numbers.** Usually, you will find it hits a resistance at a number like $4.5k and $4.55K
- **Follow the news.** Has there been any news that might affect the price? Has a country just denounced exchanges or banned cryptocurrency? Is there the chance of a fork in Bitcoin or Ethereum? The news can give you a good idea of what might happen with the price of your investment. In this volatile crypto space, many bigger news have effect on the price short-term. However, this is not always the case. For instance, not long ago there were two big news about gaming platform Steam backing out from Bitcoin after a long time. Also, mining market called NiceHash got hacked for over 70million worth of Bitcoins, yet the market completely ignored it.
- **Everyone gets free coins when a cryptocurrency forks.** When Bitcoin forked into Bitcoin Cash, everyone who held Bitcoin was given 1 Bitcoin Cash for every Bitcoin that they held. This will happen every time Bitcoin forks, but you must have a holding in Bitcoin at the time of the capture date in the fork.
- **Don't go chasing free coins.** At the time of writing, 1 Bitcoin Cash has a value of over $1600 while Bitcoin is valued at just under $10, 000. If you lose hundreds, even thousands just to get 1 Bitcoin Cash for free, it really isn't worth it. Many altcoins have rallied even up to 5-10x in prices very quickly. Don't buy in when something is already overhyped and up. The market usually has

predictable cycles - once a coin has 5-10x its previous price, it will likely pull-back for shortly. These "free coins" are often scams or very small in terms of value. Or forks (like Bitcoin cash).

- **Reality check:** In crypto markets, even three-digit returns have proven to be quite common. Don't get lost in the continuous returns in hopes of eternal free money. The current bull market can't remain forever, so focus on the value it brings and the current valuation of each crypto vs. its market cap. i.e., do research before investing.
- **Do your research.** Always do your own research before blindly investing in "X" coin or platform. Before investing (preferably any coin), consider **at least** following:

- Market cap: i.e. Bitcoin 200billion & Ethereum 70b etc.
- Current price: i.e. Bitcoin 10 000$ & Ethereum 450$ etc.
- Supply: 20million or 20billion?
- Bitcoin 21million & Ethereum 100~million
- Developers behind the project, long-term potential?
- What is the purpose of this project? Does it solve an **actual** problem?
- Do they have existing time-tested product to show for **right now**?
- Does it look professional; do they have existing or future **verified** partnerships? Anything that could even remotely make the project fail?
- Do they provide source code or is it just promises?
- Is this a short or long-term investment?
- Do you like the project and its vision? If you do, you are more likely to not panic sell during bad times

- **Join forums or social media groups** that discuss cryptocurrencies just to get a sense of what is happening. Take everything with a pinch of salt, go through multiple opinions and use what you read as a directive guide, then form your opinion. This will also give you an idea how the community stands behind the coin, do they trust it?
- **Bitcoin could be knocked off the top.** It may be the top right now, but there is always a small chance that another one may take its crown sometime in the future. Something to consider if you are after the "next Bitcoin".
- **Big players can distort and control the prices.** Volume is always good on any of the cryptocurrency exchanges but don't mistake this for trading stocks and shares. If you were playing about with 100 Bitcoin, for example, and you tried to sell or buy 100 at once, the market will more than likely be distorted. Take the time to watch the exchanges, watch the buy and sell orders. Notice that when the sell volume goes up, the price drops and when the buy orders are up, the price will rise. If you have capital, it won't be difficult to make the price go up or down. Stick to buying and selling in average volumes. Also, look out for pump and dumps. These may look like many people selling in one go but they could well be one person or investment group messing about with the price by dumping massive amounts of coins. The lack of any regulation may well be a blessing in some respects; in others, it is a curse.
- **Learn the language.** It's no good trying to invest or trade if you don't understand even the most common of terms. You will also find it easier to get together with others in the crypt forums if you understand the basic

terms and words. (remember the **vocabulary** in beginning for most basic terms)
- **Know when taking a loss is the right thing to do.** It's no fun, but if you went short and didn't put a stop in, it might be more sensible for some individuals to take that loss and wait for the price to recover again
- **Know what you are putting your money into** and understand the risks. All cryptocurrencies are highly volatile, some more, some less and purchasing Bitcoin at near to, say $9500 means purchasing it at near to its highest ever price. Those who predicted Bitcoin would reach $10,000 are so far right, but it could so easily plummet in price. Don't buy into all-time highs.
- **Bitcoin is not the blockchain.** Too many people confuse the two, but they are both different things – Bitcoin is the currency, while the blockchain is the revolutionary technology it is built on.
- **Fiat currency has not disappeared.** Bitcoin is not legal tender in many places, and neither are any other cryptocurrencies. The banks are somewhat more suspicious of them than we are. Understandably since Bitcoin is one of their greatest treats in history at the moment. Get caught up in the craze, and you might find it easy to forget that and right now the governments are the ones with the power – it is a risky business betting against them.
- **Don't be discouraged.** There sure is a lot to consider when it comes to investing, it may even appear boring, but as with everything in life, you just have to *do it*, to get the full grasp on how things work. Everything has to start from somewhere, right? After all, nobody really knows

what will happen in the future. Blockchain could revolutionize the world as we know it, but we have to wait and see.
- **Don't be an idiot, use common sense.** May sound offensive, but it is often times lacking. Please think before you act. Many people let emotions guide their "investing." I trust you will be fine, after all you did pick up *this book and* you've been reading up until here.

"Be fearful when others are greedy and greedy when others are fearful" -Warren Buffett

One memorable rule of thumb I heard of was along these lines: "if you're having too much fun investing, you're not investing, you're gambling. Which is fine as long as long you realize and can afford it." Now, this doesn't apply directly to crypto, since you will likely experience all kind of emotions but you get the point, right? Whenever you are taking advice on "X" coin, remember to think for yourself: what does the other party benefit from me buying this coin? Almost all of the advice regarding a specific coin is at least somewhat biased, never take advice from only one person and form your own educated opinion. I can't stress this enough. *The only exception being of course this holy book.*

Think of it this way- You heard about a big car race. It is really fast, lots of people race in it, some people have lots of experience on the track, some are legit professional drivers, others are just starting out, but everyone is on the same track. Some people have really fast cars with lots of gizmos and gadgets, others have old beat up slow cars (the beginners in this scenario). Now there is a lot of money to win if you can drive fast and good, and sometimes just your luck will get you through, but even more important than a fast car and lots of luck is knowing how to drive your own car and navigate the track. What many of the beginners are doing here is entering the race, losing the race, and blaming it on someone else. For example, a person that was giving them some friendly advice before the race (of which you should ALWAYS take with a grain of salt). But then come to find out they didn't even have the time to get in the car in the first place and do their own driving when the race was going on. Basically, if you're trying to race with the big players you need to learn to drive on your own, and more importantly have the time to do so. This is why the long-term; "buy and forget about it" is such a great strategy for the most of us. How do you think most of the people that bought Bitcoin back in 2011 were able to hold onto it? I would guess that the majority of them just plain forgot about it for a while, hence why you need small enough position to not waste time worrying about it.

ICOs and chapter summary

All of this advice goes for all cryptocurrencies, not only Bitcoin, but especially the small cryptocurrencies. Altcoins usually follow Bitcoin on good days and lose out **big time** on the bad days. Funnily enough often referred and "shitcoins" by the existing community for being practically nonexistent.

An ICO is an initial coin offering where you basically give the "project" Bitcoin or Ether in reward of these coins they offer, that are just like most of the existing coins, perceived value. It is somewhat similar to IPO of stocks if you are familiar with them. Generally, after few weeks or months these ICOs are then offered as brand-new altcoins in some of the exchanges or inside their website – there may be value in them but It's much tougher to get that value than it is to get it from the tried and tested Bitcoin or other established coins.

Initial coin sales may be an interesting option for those willing to risk a lot more for greater returns. I will absolutely say that you should not even consider investing in ICOs if you are new to cryptocurrencies. First, learn the basics properly. Always remember to analyze and research everything extremely carefully before investing. You must be confident with your investment position! The ICO investment returns can vary a lot. They could either: 1. Eventually 10-1000x~ your initial investment (100x+ is obviously incredibly rare, a lot of knowledge and luck is needed) 2. More likely: **Lose absolutely everything** or most of your initial investment. Thing with ICOs is that it is rather simple to create one, leading to **at least 99%** of them to be either scams or fail on the long run. Catching the big fish is very hard, since the competition is massive.

While few of them will be success stories, most will be scams or just crash and burn. ICOs are not regulated so there's no guarantee whatsoever, they could vanish at any time, often in their white paper it is stated that the coins are worthless and they can't be held responsible. Often times the token metrics of these ICOs are dangerously similar to the dot-com boom. In other words, the project managers will make money even if the project fails long-term since they are usually looking to raise millions for the "blockchain company" that is built around an imaginary problem. What's exactly driving all the prices up then? Greed and speculation. Of course, if you strongly believe in certain coin and fully acknowledge the risks, then go for it. There are many ICOs giving you great short-term returns even when their project is poor.

Blockchain projects are actually doing worse than the dot com bubble in general. Quick statistics on cryptocurrencies versus dot-com companies indicates approximately 8% of all cryptocurrencies launched to this day are still operating (number based on the research of China Academy of Information & Communications, CAICT). Most estimations suggest there's been over 4000 cryptocurrencies in total (most created in the past few years). However, 48% of dot-com companies survived through 2004. (according to: https://en.wikipedia.org/wiki/Dot-com_bubble) April 2018

The definition of "being alive" is somewhat vague but most of the time cryptocurrency is alive as long as it has active developers improving the project.

Now that the ICO sales pitch is out the way. Let's summarize everything up. Buy at the low prices, sell at the high prices; use an exchange and make use of limit orders as soon as possible.

Be conservative and don't throw your entire life savings at it. Remember, for most of us "buy and forget" is a great option. More importantly, never expect that you will know it all. We all have different opinions. Don't throw money that you don't have or can't afford to lose, try to discover your realistic risk tolerance as early as possible. It makes sense here, but unfortunately, there are always people that will "invest" beyond their capabilities. There's a lot of small variables that you need to always look at and consider in order to maximize your chances. At the end of the day I'd suggest to regularly take off some profits back to fiat money later, so eventually, you'd be playing with profits only, I mean unless you're mentally prepared to lose it all at worst.

Still following? Great, and also surprising. No worries... I will be dropping more brilliant pieces of knowledge & wisdom in the remaining chapters. Do not forget to implement at least some of the tips and ideas I just listed.

Chapter 10: How do I get Cryptocurrency?

Ready to get some Bitcoin for yourself? Maybe participate in some other blockchain project? Whether it's 0.01 or 1BTC, I recommend mainly long-term holdings in this book as I hope by now you are at least a bit interested in cryptos and especially the blockchain for the long-term. Long-term is also relative in case you make a gain of 3x your initial investment, you could consider taking some profits out for instance. This is the ideal way for beginners to start investing. Buy a very small fraction of a Bitcoin or Ethereum at first to see how it works. Recall the possible potential of this technology, it's still very early so don't rush it. Focus on understanding the process before buying anything.

Now try to recall some of the earlier chapter's advice. Feel free to get back to the previous chapter if needed. Also, this isn't some "guru advice" so in case you have more background in trading or short-term investing, sure go for it. Cryptocurrencies are currently incredibly beneficial for a trader that knows what they are doing.

Before we get to the best cryptocurrency trading platforms, let's clarify some things first. What is the point of a cryptocurrency exchange? You are always buying from another individual, who is selling them. All the exchange does is provide a safe and simple environment to trade. They guarantee that buyers get their bitcoins and sellers get their money at agreed price. There are countless different cryptocurrency trading/exchange sites. Even some stock broker platforms offer blockchain and cryptocurrency based stocks. However, we want to stay as safe as possible, so all the exchanges listed are essentially industry leaders.

Getting started there isn't really any other more reliable sites. Also, I don't want to bore you with an endless listing of pretty much similar sites. On a final note, usually, you're required to provide verified ID so be prepared to verify your identity in order to unlock any meaningful features. Many sites require it before you even start (IDs such as passport, driver's license, photo ID).

Now for the final chapters, this is where the practical guidance slash information part begins. The following chapters will give you basic practical concept on how buying, storing and using cryptos actually works. Go through the next chapters normally but remember there is an actual guide at the end of this book.

Examples of what to look for when choosing your broker(s):

- Safety. How satisfied are their customers? Do the vast majority enjoy their service? Is the site considered to be trustworthy? Is their data being transparent? Are they properly regulated? And so on. (there are countless of smaller centralized yet unregulated exchanges out there)
- Which altcoins do they offer? (every broker pretty much has Bitcoin and Ethereum)
- What type of fees do they charge? (are you looking to be trading more actively or long-term holding)

Coinbase:

If you are somewhat familiar with cryptocurrencies, you may have heard of Coinbase. A multi-billion-dollar company. Coinbase is currently the most popular crypto exchange provider. Coinbase is undeniably the simplest cryptocurrency provider. They have by far the most beginner friendly site design helping you to get started. If you are really new to this whole cryptocurrency concept I'd definitely suggest trying out

Coinbase first. You are also quite limited with the starting options since you will need to deposit some fiat ($), to convert into Bitcoin. More on this later.

Now you may think Coinbase is the perfect choice, right? For a beginner, I'd say absolutely! Even later on you want to keep your Coinbase account as a sort of shifting tool between fiat money and cryptocurrencies. However, their big downside is considerably big fees and limited coin supply. Bitcoin, Ethereum, and Litecoin. It's announced that they will add more coins in the future. You should use Coinbase as a beginner to quickly get more comfortable with cryptos or for long-term hold purchases and fiat money transfers. Definitely the easiest option for a simple purchase. If you are not yet interested on any more complicated exchanges, you may skip the next headlines: Binance & Minor exchanges.

Don't want to put all your eggs in one basket? Want to explore more than just currencies like Bitcoin and Litecoin? Here are some other great brokers covering multiple smaller cryptocurrencies, platforms and industry-specific based cryptocurrencies.

Binance:

I've left a separate Binance tutorial on the enhancement. Here you can register first really easily without any extra IDs. You start off with "level 1" verification which allows you to trade up to 2Bitcoins a day. Later on, you can later provide ID verification in order to upgrade your withdrawal limits if needed. For two-factor authentication, you are required to download Google authentication app to use Binance as an international user. Using two-factor authentications is really important with any online broker. Google Auth. App is very simple and secure, and you just download it from the app store. Always make sure you download the official apps which are proven and have millions of users. Unfortunately, with Binance they support only Chinese mobile numbers with direct SMS. With Coinbase you can use direct SMS verification. If this all sounds new, no worries. Go and preferably test around these features yourself before you actually start buying any crypto.

This exchange also has interesting giveaways and ongoing events, which isn't that common amongst the biggest exchanges.

Really clear site in general, comprehensive selection of the biggest cryptocurrencies (more than 100), the only confusing part is understanding the exchange. Just look around and learn the main currencies trading acronyms, like BTC (Bitcoin), ETH (Ethereum/Ether), LTC (Litecoin), etc. I will leave some more on the pdf. BNB on Binance is their own coin (Binance coin).

Once you have setup an account on an exchange that has multiple markets, you will need to understand how to actually buy between different crypto markets. More on this later.

Minor exchanges:

Basically similar sites with the previously mentioned, but with a bunch of more altcoins, and higher entry barrier, which could be confusing for a beginner. But, if you are interested in some specific newer altcoin, feel free to search for alternative exchanges, you could begin by looking at coinmarketcap.com. Every exchange has their strengths and weaknesses, but the exchange itself isn't necessarily important unless they don't have the cryptocurrency you want to buy or you are planning to hold your cryptocurrencies on the exchange. More on this later

Again, you can other safe exchange services yourself but in such case make sure to research the exchange before using it. All sites mentioned have international support and user base.

General note whenever you are sending cryptocurrency, Bitcoin for example, don't send Bitcoin to Litecoin wallet and vice versa, because it will not work. When sending Bitcoin from one address to another, always use the same currency. The exchanges are for when you want to switch between cryptocurrencies, or you can just sell a part of Bitcoin to USD for instance, and then buy Litecoin when needed. If this is confusing, again don't worry. You will get it with experience. Just remember to send BTC to BTC address.

A lot to process here. Don't overthink the broker as you can change it easily later on. Pick one and start getting familiar with them. Browse the site for a couple days, look at their guides, or search videos on YouTube for demonstration etc. As I said, Coinbase is most likely your best bet if you are a beginner. But as you progress, start to experiment with different exchanges. As a good rule of thumb, you should start to look for alternative ways of storing your cryptocurrency once you decide to hold any coin or a large sum of coins for a while that you can't afford to lose. Practical guidance on the PDF enhancement.

Although none of the centralized public exchanges out there is absolutely bulletproof, I'd strongly recommend against using or holding funds on the following exchange: Bitfinex, and the cryptocurrency: Tether. Simply, there is just enormous evidence against them, implying it is unfortunately blatant money laundering scheme. I will mention this again on the enhancement in more detail.

Stock brokers and blockchain-related stocks:

Many regular stock brokers offer shares of blockchain based companies, which some may find more appropriate to invest. Investor considering direct "blockchain stocks" as an option, should perform just as much research on the different companies as when investing into cryptocurrencies. This does not mean buying any share containing the word blockchain in it.

Great example of the foolish market behavior within these so called "blockchain stocks" is Long Island Iced Tea Corp. Corporation focused on ice tea has officially changed its name to

Long Blockchain Corp. The ice tea maker is now focusing on pa partnering with in blockchain-related companies. This was only an announcement, yet the company shares almost tripled in value after the announcement. If you were to invest into blockchain related stocks, the best bet would definitely be on a company that is more directly involved with the blockchain development. This does show a huge interest and speculation in blockchain at the given time however it does resemble similarities to the notorious dot com boom. Alternatively, you could pick up stocks that are likely to benefit from the mainstream implementation of blockchain technology.

Lately popular US based stock exchange Robinhood announced its upcoming cryptocurrency services, who knows we could possibly see more traditional stock brokers starting to launch their own cryptocurrency exchanges. On the other hand, we could also see many stock brokers refusing to work with cryptocurrencies due to their highly volatile nature that is not common for the traditional stock market. Many traditional companies realized just how much money the bigger crypto exchanges such as Binance have been making, hence why some of the traditional banks have been working on crypto index funds, even rumors for a Nasdaq crypto ETF in the future (exchange traded fund, multiple currencies in one).

Centralized vs. decentralized exchanges

Blockchain and cryptocurrencies were envisioned as community-oriented open-source initiatives where the participants of a decentralized network have the power instead of a central authority like a bank or government for instance. This has held mostly true with the exception of development teams that still have a significant say in the project. Often times many of the altcoin blockchains have a leader that everyone believes in and follows, somewhat limiting the effects of complete decentralization, however, for many it is not necessarily that big of a deal.

Centralized exchanges however, are the exact opposite of what has been mentioned above—there is a direct conflict between what they represent and blockchain values. A centralized exchange (ex. Coinbase, Binance, etc.) is run by a profit-oriented company that gets revenue from their platform's fee structures. To put it simply: both the buying and selling into the current blockchain ecosystem require fees—all of which go to centralized exchanges. For instance, Coinbase reported over 2 million daily earnings at its peak.

Greatest benefit using decentralized exchanges is the fact that you are in control all the time. Other benefits include anonymity, practically any registered token on market and 100% server uptime since they work directly with smart contracts in the blockchain. Unfortunately, though, these exchanges need a lot more development before they are attractive to the average user. They are very hard to use in general as they work directly with the blockchain. As of now all decentralized exchanges are unable to transfer fiat ($) to cryptocurrencies, making them rather unpractical for the average user. However, decentralized exchanges definitely have a bright future ahead. For some enthusiastic residents decentralized exchanges may seem appealing, especially for those individuals experiencing uncertain legal conditions regarding the future ownership of cryptocurrencies. Decentralized exchanges have the highest level of entry for newcomers. Example on decentralized exchange: https://idex.market This one is running on the Ethereum blockchain. You can look it up just to see how crude these decentralized exchanges are at the moment. It kind of reminds me of the early windows messenger, which was replaced by Skype, which then was somewhat replaced by Discord (or WhatsApp vs. texting). What's next?

All the resources for these exchanges and more can be found in the end on a separate PDF guide. Do you remember the mining concept? Great, because the next chapter will focus on cryptocurrency mining and staking, giving you a basic idea about the different mining systems and should you consider doing it yourself. Now might be a good time to take a break or grab a cup of coffee... we are about to get a bit technical. Again...

Chapter 11: Digital Gold Mining

Imagine mining gold. There's limited supply at which you can acquire more, and over time it will get more and more difficult to find new gold while eventually, it ends completely.

With Bitcoin and most other cryptocurrencies, the basic idea is the same. Except, again we are talking about mining digitally of course, not literal mining. Right, you probably got that. Mining yourself isn't necessarily something I would recommend anymore, but I will present you the basics. In any case, it's important to understand the concept even if you're not looking to mine yourself, because it will help you understand one of the most fundamental aspects of cryptocurrencies.

This chapter will focus only on mining principles, future and progress - how you can start mining yourself without any equipment, and how the different mining methods work. Again, I've included the links into the PDF attachment if you're interested.

During the first years of Bitcoin's creation, you could have mined Bitcoin with just your computer's processor. However, as Bitcoin got more recognition and value, people discovered that graphics cards used for gaming were way more efficient in the mining process. This eventually led to the creation of ASICs. ASICs are computers designed for one thing and one thing only - Mining Bitcoins. Ever since, the difficulty to mine more Bitcoin has gradually gotten higher and higher. This has caused mining to be less profitable for individual miners especially when you consider all the hustle required to set up a proper miner.

At the moment, the mining reward is 12.5 Bitcoin for each discovered block, which is distributed between a bunch of miners depending on how much "work" they did. This will halve when 210,000 blocks have been mined, and this is expected to happen around 2020. With the current proof of work system, you may wonder when will the last Bitcoin be mined? In the case of block halving frequency remaining around four years, it's estimated that the final Bitcoin to be mined is around 2140.

What happens when all the Bitcoins are mined? This is something we can't know for certain, but there are few possible scenarios. Bitcoin being still around in 2140~would most likely mean it being so valuable that even the transaction fees alone would encourage the mining process. Secondly, which probably is more likely, Bitcoin technology in 100 years has evolved so much that the current mining will be replaced. More on the already existing alternatives later.

Bitcoin mining is based on a system called "proof-of-work" – this means that, for any block to be added to the blockchain, a complex mathematical algorithm must be solved. Once the complex mathematical algorithm has been solved, the computer solving it receives a small reward. This reward is dependent on which coin's algorithm you are mining. Proof of work mining is the very first type of mining, used in Bitcoin and many other similar cryptocurrencies. In proof of work mining, the miners (computers solving algorithms) are the ones confirming transactions in the Bitcoin blockchain, keeping the network running. The more miners there are, the more secure the network becomes. When there is too much traffic for the network it results into relatively slow and expensive transactions within the Bitcoin network, which created need for a better solution. Lightning network is currently being developed and tested as the solution to Bitcoin's current block scaling issue. It is estimated to be applied fully between 2018-2019.

Now here's just a few basic examples, mining Bitcoin's algorithm is known as SHA-256, and you are rewarded with Bitcoin. Litecoin's algorithm is based on Scrypt and obviously the reward is Litecoin. Mining other coins than Bitcoin isn't very profitable, that is, if you invested the money directly in buying the coins. You would most likely be better off buying and holding the coin itself than making the hustle to setup its mining. Proof of work mining is the current way to mine more coins for most of the cryptocurrencies. However, it has been losing its popularity lately to mining concept called "proof of stake", more on that later. Now we will have a look at the downsides of "PoW" method.

Genesis Mining's mining farm located in Iceland:

As you can see, "proof of work" mining is not environment-friendly. Even though many of the bigger miners are using renewable energy sources, it is still going to have huge energy costs if the proof of work mining rises on the global scale. This is a double-edged sword though. Assuming Bitcoin was used on global scale with renewable energy, the mining would not necessarily act as an "energy waster", since the same issue would apply to the traditional currencies as well. Anyhow, this book isn't about the climate change or energy consumption. We'll quickly go through these issues so you'll gain a better understanding of the different algorithms.

Between 2017-2018 Bitcoin mining alone accounts for approximately 0.1% of global electricity consumption. Not only this, but many claim it will eventually corrupt the markets as it is pretty centralized. Bitcoin's mining power is heavily controlled by the biggest mining company. Same argument could be said to the distribution of Bitcoins, but this distribution is rather similar to USD in the end of the day. The issue with Bitcoin's current mining distribution is definitely controversial subject and even the core mining algorithm is a subject for change. PoW is technically essential for decentralization (at the moment), but in practice all the power is distributed on these big miners constantly creating more coins. Therefore, gaining more influence and control over the prices later, along with the wealthier investors. There has been discussion on changing Bitcoin's mining algorithm in the future, but whenever there is a proposal for bigger changes, it takes long time to reach any type of consensus. However, there are many existing projects such as Cardano, EOS and Ethereum's future vision to have the issue fixed. This solution is called "Proof of Stake" instead. There are some early implementations already existing with the "PoS" technology. Another technology claiming to fix the issue is currently known as Hashgraph, which is very different to traditional blockchains, as well as many more early developments. However, it's still too early and vague to be viewed here.

Proof of Stake algorithm (PoS) is an alternate way of verifying and validating the transaction or block. Make no mistake here, PoS technically consumes energy as well, but arguably in a smarter way. In proof of stake the algorithm will pick the validator (Equivalent of "miner" in the Proof of Work) by the amount of stake(coins) a validator has in their wallet and the respective age of the stake. If you have 100,000 alt coins (let us say X-coin which uses PoS) in a wallet, it will have an age attached to it on how long you have it. Here the 100,000 X-coins is the stake. If you move your coins from one address (or wallet) to another, the aging gets reset. This amount is like the security deposit which means the Validator holds a significant stake in X-coin with good aging will gain a higher chance to validate a block. Once a block is validated, the reward is distributed to the stake holders. This allows building a trusted and distributed network with loyal Validators (high stake of coins). The Validators earn part of or the whole transaction fee.

In PoS, it is not mining but forging which is done by the Validator who will process and forge a block to the chain. This eliminates the below challenges from PoW and is believed to have an advantage. Basic concept is relatively same on all the different PoS models. The major projects running on PoS have slightly different algorithms, just like Bitcoin and Litecoin have different PoW algorithm.

(source: https://www.cardanohub.org/en/the-daedalus-wallet/) *9.12.2017*

Basically, if you are familiar with dividend stocks, proof of stake is essentially cryptocurrency version of a dividend stock or passive income. You'd put your coins into a special staking wallet where they earn X amount of coins by validating transactions on the network. This amount and frequency of earned coins varies greatly from; 1.) Amount of coins being staked 2.) Which type of specific proof of stake system the cryptocurrency is using. For instance, 2,5,10% annual returns of the amount of coins being staked. The model is still very recent and therefore not yet time-tested like Bitcoin. In other words, choosing the most optimal distribution of coins without sacrificing security or decentralization is difficult.

Mining keeps the fundamentals running. It is very likely that the existing mining algorithms will constantly be improved upon, which is why you should take different mining algorithms with a pinch of salt. *Back in the day you could have just picked up rusty pickaxe and start mining, why is this so complicated...* Now we are going to take a look on how the cryptocurrency storing progress is done, and the most ideal ways to store and secure your cryptocurrency.

Chapter 12: Storing Your Cryptocurrency

Let's begin by understanding how you even exactly store these currencies. **Cryptocurrency wallet** = Software program that stores private and public keys and interacts with various blockchains to enable users to send and receive digital currency and observe their balance. In order to use Bitcoin or any other cryptocurrency, you will need a digital cryptocurrency wallet.

Most exchanges like Coinbase and Binance have their own built-in digital wallets where you can store your first cryptocurrency, recommended only temporarily unless it's a very small amount you are not worried about. Different coins have different options when it comes to wallets, the majority of cryptos have all the options while some tiny new coin may have fewer storing option.

The technology and options behind these different wallets are constantly being developed further. The user interface with wallets outside of exchange does leave a lot to be desired. Be sure to not ignore the storing part, although you may not find this to be the most interesting process, it's very important to stay safe and secure your cryptocurrencies properly. Really simplified, it is the internet version of a wallet. Again, we have the same problem as with choosing the broker platform. There are numerous different wallets available, each being somewhat different with their unique features.

Now that you have very basic idea of these wallets, why would you want one? It keeps you safe. Let me explain more. In the following examples we are going to use Bitcoin and Coinbase. You may be confused. For example; *"What do I need a wallet for, I just want me some Bitcoin!"* First things first. As a beginner, when you are just learning and investing to get started, it's perfectly fine to keep your Bitcoin in Coinbase or any other cloud broker that you choose. However, it is important to understand the basic way in securing your cryptocurrencies outside the built-in exchange addresses. After all, "being your own bank" is one of the key purpose of blockchain. I will try to keep this short (probably not).

Bob has 10 Bitcoins in his Coinbase account sitting there waiting for Bitcoin's price to increase. He has kept those Bitcoins there for a year with hard earned money he absolutely can't afford to lose. Bob follows Bitcoin's price and news every day, he is passionate about the future. He considers himself to be an expert. He never told his carefully thought password to anyone. He is planning to buy a new car with his Bitcoin profits. Then suddenly one-day Bob checks the account balance and it shows zero. Some of Coinbase's addresses have been leaked during maintenance and hacked. Bob's address unfortunately being one of them, and the coins are gone. In the best case he may be able to recover them depending on the broker, but he obviously doesn't want to count on that, and it turns out he actually had a weak password without two-factor mobile authentication enabled.

How could this happen? Other than Bob having a shitty password without extra authentications covering his 10Bitcoins. Default exchange cloud online wallets such as Coinbase have to store your private keys online in order to provide you the built-in exchange address, which makes it possible for a hacker to attack. This can be prevented up to a great degree with a strong password and 2-step authentication, but as you can see, it's definitely not a smart idea to store, let's say 100 Bitcoins (about million dollars) in your Coinbase or any other cloud wallet. Since whenever you have the funds in an exchange address you are essentially trusting your money on them, because with your private key on hand the exchange can control your funds however they want. Being not much different from a regular bank account. When the core idea of cryptocurrencies is to avoid the concentration of power in the hands of huge behemoths. More on setting up the mobile 2FA and other practicalities in the PDF guide.

Here's what to look for when choosing your wallet(s):

- Cost. Is it free or not? Does it make sense for me to use & setup an expensive wallet if I have 0.05 Bitcoins?
- Security. How important is it for you to be in full control?
- Mobility and practicality. How easy is it to move, where and when can I access it?
- User-friendliness. How easy it is to use.

So, you have acquired considerable amount of cryptocurrency. You can't wait to lose them? I mean... can't afford to lose them, right? It would be the time to get a wallet. You don't, great because now we are only going through the different wallet types. Understanding the wallets gives you an idea what to do when you may actually need one outside of the exchange.

Next, we are looking at the existing wallet types and the major differences to know. Specific information on each wallet can be found on the respective websites. It should be noted: **always confirm** the external services before putting any money into them.

Online wallet: These are all the different wallets you have with different cloud services. Your online brokers like Coinbase, Binance, as well as separate online wallet providers like myetherwallet.com for instance. A fine choice if you have a small amount of crypto for more regular use and you have a strong password with 2-step authentication required. Very beginner-friendly and easy practical solution.

Examples of online wallets:

Cloud service sites where you own the keys: Blockchain wallet, StrongCoin, myetherwallet etc.

Exchange wallets where the respective exchange owns the keys: Centralized exchanges such as, Coinbase, Binance, Bitstamp, Gemini etc.

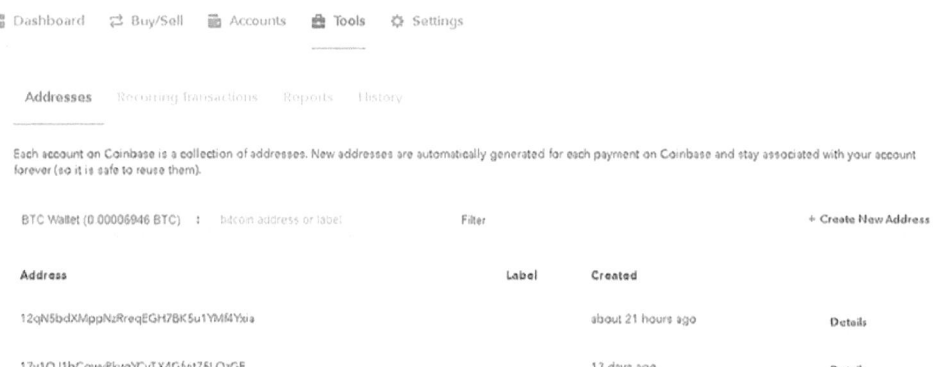

Every centralized exchange has automatically generated address and whenever you make a purchase it shows up automatically on the balance of your account. As you can see with Coinbase you can create additional different addresses for Bitcoin, Ethereum and Litecoin really easily. Making it very attractive for a beginner. Other exchanges have generally just one default address for each cryptocurrency and you can't generate more addresses. Although the amount of addresses doesn't necessarily matter since they automatically show you the combined amount even if you have funds on four different addresses in your Coinbase account. It is important to understand however, using wallets outside of exchange is different as you will not have combined funds through different addresses like with Coinbase.

Sites like www.myetherwallet.com/ are also online wallets, but the main difference is that the separate online wallet providers do **not** store your private key (private key was, essentially to have the full control over sending the funds) like the exchanges do. Myetherwallet can be used for Ethereum, including all the ERC20 tokens built on Ethereum that many existing tokens and ICOs use. More on this in the enhancement. Myetherwallet is also compatible with the hardware wallets like Ledger and Trezor, making it one of the best current sources. Using these is more complicated, but worth it if you are looking to stay safe and remain in full control over your crypto. For Bitcoin you could use online blockchain wallet, www.blockchain.com or StrongCoin, https://strongcoin.com. Along with hardware wallets of course.

As stated previously the only major difference between actual online wallets and exchange wallets is the ownership of the private key. Online wallets are definitely the easiest target for hackers, especially the exchange ones. Next, you will learn about the more secure options for larger amounts of cryptocurrencies. With online wallets, eventually it comes down to personal preference. Again, if you are completely new to cryptocurrencies take it slow. It is okay to keep small amount of funds on an exchange at first.

Mobile wallet: This wallet is basically an app you can download to your phone. You can obviously use them anywhere with your phone. They are pretty secure, some have multi-signature accesses, and you can even return the wallet if you lose your phone. However, these are not the ideal way to store large amount of funds.

Examples of mobile wallets:

Bread Wallet
+; Privacy, security, beginner friendly and free

-; No web or desktop options, lacks some features and only for Bitcoins

Mycelium
+; Privacy, advanced security, many features, open source software and free, plans or already has some altcoins
-; No web or desktop options, not beginner friendly

Jaxx
+; Privacy, advanced security, many features, open source software, free, has multiple currency options, user-friendly
-; Code not open source, sometimes slow

(they are for Android & iPhone)

Hardware wallet: These are different in a sense that they are actual physical devices like USB. Hardware wallets are stored offline and have really high security. This is an ideal option for anyone with significantly high crypto possession. If you don't want to have any risks whatsoever, this is the best option. You generate the keys during an initialization procedure. Funds stored through the hardware wallet are not directly in the device, but in the blockchain, the device acts only as a "key" to accessing your funds.

Example hardware wallets:

Ledger Nano S

Price: 70~$
+; Multi currency support, 3rd-party apps, relatively cheap, very simple / beginner-friendly and has backup
-; Slightly clumsy management
(however, unfortunately most of the user interface around cryptocurrency and blockchain is rather clumsy for the average

user with non-tech background as the technology is still being developed)

Trezor
Price: 100$~
+; Really high security, open source software, beginner-friendly, in-built screen
-; Slightly more expensive

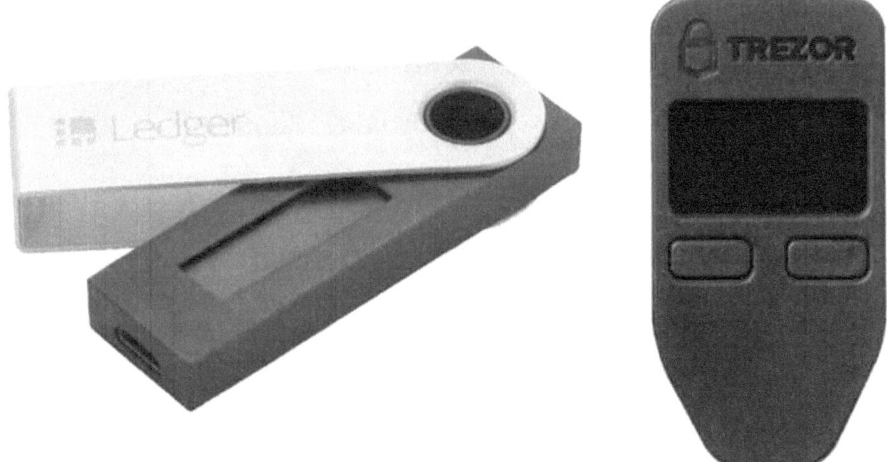

Paper wallet: Easy to use and high security level. You basically store your private keys and public address by printing it into a piece of paper that therefore grants you access to your funds on the blockchain. Transferring any digital currency to your paper wallet is accomplished by the transfer of funds from your software wallet to the public address shown on your paper wallet. To print a paper wallet, you must have your funds stored on a decentralized wallet where you own the private key. For instance, Ethereum on myetherwallet.com.

This term of paper wallet refers to physical paper copy or printout of your public and private keys. It can also refer to a piece of software that is used to securely generate the keys that you then print into paper. These wallets aren't necessarily the most practical for the everyday usage, but then again right now there isn't that many services you can realistically be buying with Bitcoins. Ideally, you'd want to store all long-term funds on either hardware or paper wallet, or both because they are the only way to keep your funds "offline".

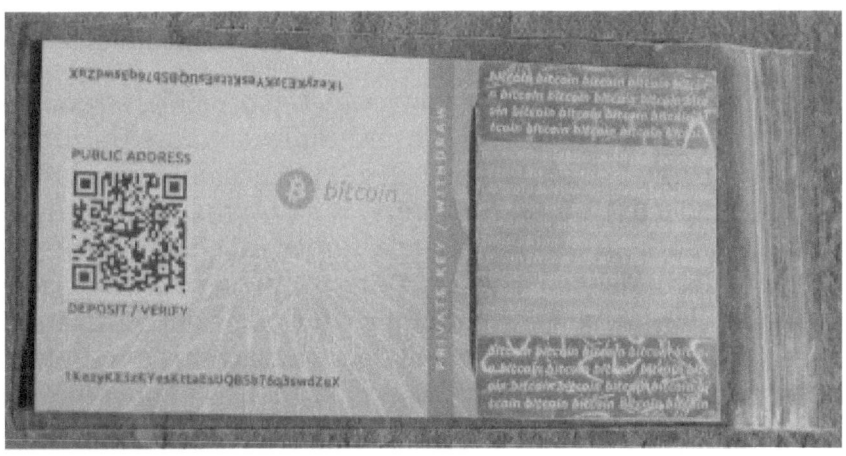

Bitcoin paper wallet. Public address and the private key. (they look different)

Recently as the value of cryptocurrencies increased, more and more thieves started phishing for private keys out of uninformed owners. They are called "public" and "private" for a reason. Remember private key is the one granting you access to your crypto, don't share it!

Recap of chapter 12

As I said if you are beginner, let's say you buy 0.03 Bitcoin for 200$ to speculate and you're not planning to do anything else for now. You will be better off just keeping the other wallets in mind until you get more involved. Who knows... maybe that 0.03 Bitcoin is worth 2000$ someday, maybe now it would be a better time to consider other options? Of course, you can plan ahead but it requires just a bit more time and effort. More examples and little bit more practical details owning cryptocurrencies can be found on the enhancement.

Always remember to back up your wallet, if possible, so you can access it in case it gets lost. Hardware wallets require this during the initialization process. You will get the backup information from the respective wallet providers. With online wallets, always use 2-step authentications when possible, especially when you have your funds on exchange! With the bigger sites such as Coinbase they actually often require it. Google authentication app is a great example. For smaller transactions or crypto possession use online wallets (or exchanges), as of now they are the most practical and easiest option. For bigger crypto possessions and long-term investments strongly consider hardware wallets. Links are in the enhancement. This was an overview of the ways to store cryptocurrencies. Please read the guides on the respective websites before transferring funds or purchasing to make sure you will never lose anything.

Conclusion, What's Next?

I hope this book was able to help you to understand the blockchain and how it works, as well as a little more about responsibly investing in cryptocurrencies, risks, benefits, and the main research principles for any currency that you plan to invest in.

The next step is to make your own decision on cryptocurrencies and then possibly take it even further. Learn all you can about the existing coins and what they use the blockchain technology for, what can be improved etc. before you make any decision whether to invest or not.

On the whole, the blockchain technology has got huge potential, especially when it comes to providing changes on many of today's industries, such as energy distribution, advertising, privacy and a great deal more. The biggest innovation that the technology provides is the ability for participants to reliably move assets around, using the internet, without needing to get a third-party involved.

For the perspective of marketing, it helps to think of the blockchain as a kind of business process for the next generation, a process of software improvement. The blockchain, and other collaborative technologies, promise to provide us with the ability to improve current business processes that already take place between companies, causing a radical drop in the "cost of trust".

Remember that change is inevitable. Technology has never changed at such speed. What is new and innovative today, is old and replaced tomorrow.

With cryptocurrency and its current conditions, it's very likely that we are still going to see drastic changes. As the legend himself, Albert Einstein once said: *"The measure of intelligence is the ability to change"*.

We must not become overly attached to anything, in this case we can't blindly follow a coin thinking; *"this will revolutionize the world no matter what, I will never sell it"*. Or as the Buddha has said; *"attachment leads to suffering"*. (wasn't that a Sneaky way to pitch a Buddha quote)

We can't expect great results without any work. This is why my final suggestion to you is this. Actively seek for a project that provides a solution to all the current problems of the "big" coins, that is, if you are more of a high-risk high-reward seeker. But remember, Bitcoin is the number one cryptocurrency for a reason. It is also likely to stay this way, but who knows maybe the next year this time TrumpCoin or another one of the gazillion jokes or scams replaced Bitcoin. Let's give it 1 satoshi chance (0.00000001%).

There are many promising projects that you can get in very early, just like Bitcoin once was. Difficulty in this is obviously choosing the right coin as we are only speculating. I highly believe there are still many innovative projects that will shape the future big time. For instance, something big we didn't touch on this book is the upcoming shift of artificial intelligence. Even though I believe I've acquired all the latest research, facts, diversity and my most unbiased opinion I still do always recommend for you to look on other resources if you are really interested in this topic and plan to take the full advantage of early mastery.

Finally, if you found value in this book, then I'd like to ask you for a quick favor, would you have time to leave a review on Amazon.com right now?

Remember to leave a review for this book on Amazon!

Thank you! It really helps me. Constructive criticism is welcomed as well. I appreciate your efforts to learn and I'm glad I had the chance to talk to you. Thank you and I wish best of luck with your further research & success! Remember to keep on learning. You will be amazed with how much you can learn about the future. You can find the link to the PDF file next.

Observation thus far; At the end of the day I have come to a conclusion that people naturally have different risk preferences as well as views of what is and isn't going to serve a purpose. However, there is really no universal "facts" or best response when it comes to the world of cryptocurrencies. At the given moment most universally accepted facts can be found from the market. i.e. Bitcoin is number one and so on. It is subjective experiment but the future is bright.

"I do think Bitcoin is the first [encrypted money] that has the potential to do something like change the world."

- Peter Thiel, Co-Founder of PayPal

PDF enhancement

bit.ly/crypto_guide1

Still not tired of cryptocurrencies? Impressive. You might seriously be onto something... Hope you didn't just skip here. So, you want to know how to buy Bitcoin? Looking for more resources, information? In such case, please do yourself a favor and look up the guide. It will likely save you from many costly mistakes! Actually, if you made it all the way here, just check the damn guide. While going through this PDF iterate the explanation on chapters 10-12 from this book if needed to get the full grasp. It's not a virus (no guarantees though).

Feel free to share your thoughts, improvements or ask anything on email: eetusro@gmail.com

Now it's your turn. This was just the first step of the journey.

Yours, Edward Beckett

References

Andres M. Antonopoulos, The Internet of Money Kindle edition on amazon.com

Forum 1 book of history, pages 45-55, 85-97

https://bitcoin.org 2017

S. Nakamoto, whitepaper bitcoin.pdf 2009

https://www.ethereum.org/ 2017

https://www.cardanohub.org/en/the-daedalus-wallet/) December 2017

D. Pollock, https://cointelegraph.com/news/why-japan-is-best-place-to-buy-with-bitcoin first article October 2017

J. Chokun, https://99bitcoins.com/who-accepts-bitcoins-payment-companies-stores-take-bitcoins/ October, November 2017

S. Brunozzi, https://medium.com/the-naked-founder/2020-predictions-from-2017-617893fffdda November 2017

https://www.bcb.gov.br article on "origin and evolution of money" November 2017

S. Priyadarshini, http://www.preservearticles.com/2012020222471/essay-on-the-development-of-money-in-different-stages.html December 2017

https://cointelegraph.com/news/why-japan-is-best-place-to-buy-with-bitcoin

T. Rick, https://www.torbenrick.eu/blog/change-management/12-reasons-why-people-resist-change/ Meliorate change management, 2011

M. Gianpietro Zago https://medium.com/@matteozago/web-2-0-is-broken-its-time-for-a-new-paradigm-shift-2a4b1fc2ff60 January 2018

https://en.Wikipedia.org History of Money, November 2017

https://en.wikipedia.org/wiki/History_of_the_World_Wide_Web January 2018

http://futurethinkers.org/industries-blockchain-disrupt/ January 2018

https://www.cryptocompare.com/exchanges/guides/what-is-a-decentralized-exchange/ January 2018

https://medium.com/cryptomedication/uncovering-the-real-cartel-in-bitcoin-65b56a7a00a2 Chapter 10 final reference May 2018.

C. Cannucciari, Documentary: Banking on Bitcoin

W.Olszewski, Shutterstock.com

News.bitcoin.com/bitcoin-city-arnhem February 2017, chapter 7

Crypto-news.net December 2017, chapter 7

Licensed Adobe stock pictures 2017

www.ingramcontent.com/pod-product-compliance
Lightning Source LLC
Chambersburg PA
CBHW020437220526
45464CB00002B/743